Space Science

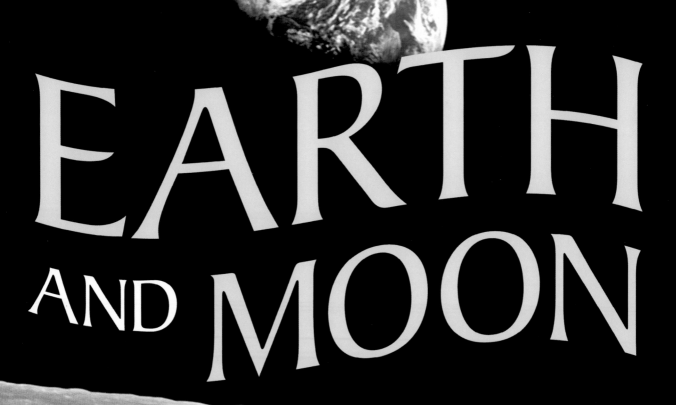

EARTH
AND MOON

How to use this book

Welcome to *Space Science*. All the books in this set are organized to help you through the multitude of pictures and facts that make this subject so interesting. There is also a master glossary for the set on pages 58–64 and an index on pages 65–72.

Photographs and diagrams have been carefully selected and annotated for clarity. Captions provide more facts.

The text is organized into chapters.

Capitals show key glossary terms. They are defined in the quick reference glossary.

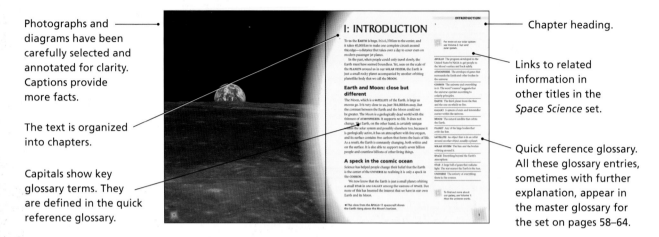

Chapter heading.

Links to related information in other titles in the *Space Science* set.

Quick reference glossary. All these glossary entries, sometimes with further explanation, appear in the master glossary for the set on pages 58–64.

 Atlantic Europe Publishing

First published in 2004 by
Atlantic Europe Publishing Company Ltd.

Copyright © 2004
Atlantic Europe Publishing Company Ltd.

Author
Brian Knapp, BSc, PhD

Art Director
Duncan McCrae, BSc

Senior Designer
Adele Humphries, BA, PGCE

Editors
Mary Sanders, BSc, and Gillian Gatehouse

Illustrations on behalf of Earthscape Editions
David Woodroffe and David Hardy

Design and production
EARTHSCAPE EDITIONS

Print
WKT Company Limited, Hong Kong

This product is manufactured from sustainable managed forests. For every tree cut down, at least one more is planted.

Space science – Volume 3: Earth and Moon
A CIP record for this book is available from the British Library

ISBN 1 86214 365 X

Picture credits
All photographs and diagrams NASA except the following:
(c=center t=top b=bottom l=left r=right)

Earthscape Editions 8t, 8–9b, 10t, 10–11b, 12–13 (*diagram*), 15b, 16b, 20b, 22, 29, 30–31 (*all*), 32–33b, 33t, 34b, 38t, 38b, 41br, 50, 55, 56–57 (*diagram*); *Paleographic Maps by Christopher R. Scotese, PALEOMAP Project, University of Texas at Arlington* 36b, 37t, 37b.

The front cover shows the first photograph of the Earth as a globe taken on the Apollo 8 mission to the Moon in December 1968; the back cover, Apollo 17 exploring the Moon's surface.

NASA, the U.S. National Aeronautics and Space Administration, was founded in 1958 for aeronautical and space exploration. It operates several installations around the country and has its headquarters in Washington, D.C.

CONTENTS

1:	**INTRODUCTION**	**4–15**
	Earth and Moon: close but different	5
	A speck in the cosmic ocean	5
	Rocky bodies	6
	Closely coupled	8
	Sidereal and synodic time	8
	The importance of gravity	9
	The seasons	10
	The phases of the Moon	13
	Eclipses	14
2:	**PLANET EARTH**	**16–41**
	The Earth in the solar system	16
	The Earth's gravity	18
	The Earth's size and shape	18
	The Earth's magnetic field	19
	The magnetosphere and the auroras	20
	The atmosphere	22
	Water on the Earth	28
	The Earth's crust	30
	Continental drift	36
	Inside the Earth	38
	Erosion on the Earth	40
	The rock cycle	40
3:	**THE MOON**	**42–57**
	The Moon's gravity	42
	The Moon's atmosphere	44
	The Moon's surface	45
	How the Moon reflects light	47
	Craters on the Moon	50
	Moon soil and Moon rock	52
	The Moon's interior	54
	Where the Moon came from	56
SET GLOSSARY		**58–64**
SET INDEX		**65–72**

▲ The Moon rising over the Earth.

1: INTRODUCTION

To us the **EARTH** is huge. It is 6,378 km to the center, and it takes 40,000 km to make one complete circuit around the edge—a distance that takes over a day to cover even on modern passenger jet planes.

In the past, when people could only travel slowly, the Earth must have seemed boundless. Yet, seen on the scale of the **PLANETS** around us in our **SOLAR SYSTEM**, the Earth is just a small rocky planet accompanied by another orbiting planetlike body that we call the **MOON**.

Earth and Moon: close but different

The Moon, which is a **SATELLITE** of the Earth, is large as moons go. It is very close to us, just 384,000 km away. But the contrast between the Earth and the Moon could not be greater. The Moon is a geologically dead world with the thinnest of **ATMOSPHERES**. It supports no life. It does not change. The Earth, on the other hand, is certainly unique within the solar system and possibly elsewhere too, because it is geologically active, it has an atmosphere with free oxygen, and its surface contains free carbon that forms the basis of life. As a result, the Earth is constantly changing, both within and on the surface. It is also able to support nearly seven billion people and countless billions of other living things.

A speck in the cosmic ocean

Science has helped people change their belief that the Earth is the center of the **UNIVERSE** to realizing it is only a speck in the **COSMOS**.

We now know that the Earth is just a small planet orbiting a small **STAR** in one **GALAXY** among the vastness of **SPACE**. But none of this has lessened the interest that we have in our own Earth and its Moon.

◄ This view from the **APOLLO** 11 spacecraft shows the Earth rising above the Moon's horizon.

For more on our solar system see Volume 2: *Sun and solar system*.

APOLLO The program developed in the United States by NASA to get people to the Moon's surface and back safely.

ATMOSPHERE The envelope of gases that surrounds the Earth and other bodies in the universe.

COSMOS The universe and everything in it. The word "cosmos" suggests that the universe operates according to orderly principles.

EARTH The third planet from the Sun and the one on which we live.

GALAXY A system of stars and interstellar matter within the universe.

MOON The natural satellite that orbits the Earth.

PLANET Any of the large bodies that orbit the Sun.

SATELLITE An object that is in an orbit around another object, usually a planet.

SOLAR SYSTEM The Sun and the bodies orbiting around it.

SPACE Everything beyond the Earth's atmosphere.

STAR A large ball of gases that radiates light. The star nearest the Earth is the Sun.

UNIVERSE The entirety of everything there is; the cosmos.

To find out more about our galaxy, see Volume 1: *How the universe works*.

In fact, rather the opposite has been the case. That is because since the first space PROBES we have been able to look down on our planet and see in it patterns and features that we never even suspected. We have realized that although we walk on its surface every day, we still know remarkably little about the Earth.

Similarly, probes and manned spaceflights have enabled us to see the Moon close up and also the side that we never see from the Earth. Dead it may be, but that has not lessened its fascination. On the contrary, we have become ever more intrigued.

Just as interesting are views of the Earth and the Moon from other planets. Here we can truly see the "blue marble," as our planet has become fondly known, set like a precious stone within the deep blackness of space.

Rocky bodies

The Earth and the Moon are so very different. But do they have anything in common? Essentially they are both rocky bodies, as opposed to ones made mainly from gas, such as Jupiter or Neptune.

In the solar system the Earth and its Moon are small and unusual. In fact, they are too small to hold in place anything more than a thin shell of gases. (Although you may have thought that the Moon has no atmosphere because astronauts wear space suits on the Moon, it does have a very thin atmosphere.) The atmospheres are also quite different from those of the gas giants, or **JOVIAN PLANETS**, in the solar system, having little hydrogen and helium, the gases that dominate these other worlds.

▶ We are now used to pictures of the Earth like this one, which shows features of the atmosphere as well as of the land and the oceans. Closeup pictures show only part of one side; they do not show the other half.

Use this picture to imagine the features of the Earth as they would be seen from space, just as we view other planets. The Earth is bright and blue, with swirling white clouds formed into belts parallel with the EQUATOR. Shining white POLES indicate snow and ice below. The growth and shrinking of the snow-covered regions through the year would also be noticeable.

The darker surface seen through the clouds is mostly ocean. It would not be easy to identify life on Earth from distant space because most inhabited areas are frequently covered by clouds.

EQUATOR The ring drawn around a body midway between the poles.

JOVIAN PLANETS An alternative group name for the gas giant planets: Jupiter, Saturn, Uranus, and Neptune.

PHASE The differing appearance of a body that is closer to the Sun, and that is illuminated by it.

POLE The geographic pole is the place where a line drawn along the axis of rotation exits from a body's surface.

PROBE An unmanned spacecraft designed to explore our solar system and beyond.

For more on the Jovian planets see Volume 5: *Gas giants*.

Closely coupled

The Earth and the Moon are bound to one another by **GRAVITY**, just as they are both bound to the **SUN**.

The **ORBIT** of the Earth around the Sun is strongly influenced by the Moon. The Earth and the Moon actually orbit the Sun around their combined **CENTER OF GRAVITY**, a point inside the Earth about 4,700 kilometers from its center. As a result, this unequal dumbbell-like pair each traces a very uneven path through space.

Sometimes the Moon is closer to the Earth (its **PERIGEE**), when it orbits at just under 360,000 km altitude. At other times it is at its greatest distance from the Earth (its **APOGEE**), when it may be almost 407,000 km from the Earth. This is due to the combined effects of the Earth, the Sun, and the other planets.

Similarly, the orbit of the Earth is influenced not just by the Sun but also by the positions of the other planets. As a result, the orbit of the Earth around the Sun is a wavy track, while the orbit of the Moon is like an open spiral.

The close coupling of the Earth and the Moon has many effects. One of the most significant is the braking effect that the Earth has had on the Moon. As a result, the Moon is in **SYNCHRONOUS ROTATION** and always faces the same way to the Earth; we never see the reverse side.

Although the Earth's spin rate is slowing down, the Earth and Moon together keep the same **MOMENTUM**. The only way for this to happen is for the Moon to move slowly away from the Earth. The result of this is that the Earth's day and month get longer.

Sidereal and synodic time

It takes 27.322 days (27 days, 7 hours, 43 minutes, and 12 seconds)—called the **SIDEREAL MONTH**—for the Earth and Moon to return to the same place against the background of the stars. But the Earth and Moon are also orbiting the Sun, and that has an important effect too.

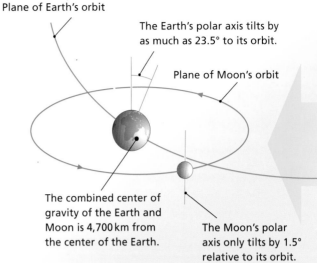

Plane of Earth's orbit

The Earth's polar axis tilts by as much as 23.5° to its orbit.

Plane of Moon's orbit

The combined center of gravity of the Earth and Moon is 4,700 km from the center of the Earth.

The Moon's polar axis only tilts by 1.5° relative to its orbit.

▲ The Earth and Moon each spin on an axis tilted to the **PLANE** containing their orbit. This diagram shows the orbit of the Moon around the Earth.

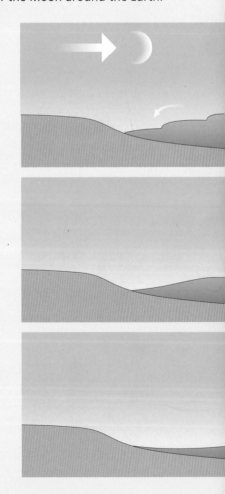

As the Earth and Moon move around the Sun, the angle of illumination changes by about 1 degree per day. The effect of this on the phases of the Moon (see pages 12–13) is to cause the time from one full Moon to the next to be 29.531 days (29 days, 12 hours, 44 minutes, and 3 seconds). This is called the **SYNODIC MONTH**.

As scientists studied the movement of the Moon, they were able to make predictions about its path and effects. Giovanni Cassini (1625–1712) discovered that the Moon's **AXIS** changes slowly over time, forming its own circular path. This change causes the Moon's phases. It also accounts for eclipses (see pages 14–15).

Johannes Kepler (1571–1630) developed a series of laws for the movement of planetary bodies, predicting that the Moon changes speed as it makes its **ECCENTRIC** orbit. That is what allows us to see nearly 60% of the Moon's surface (although not all at the same time).

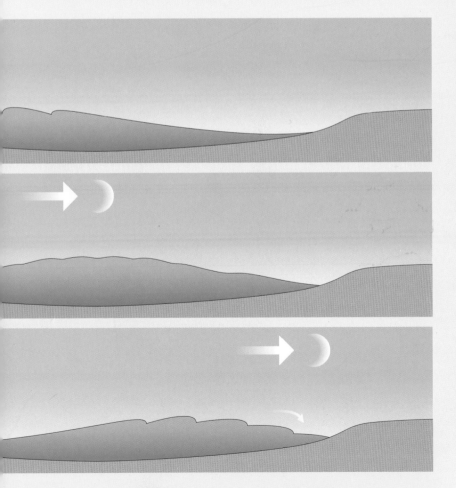

APOGEE The point on an orbit where the orbiting object is at its farthest from the object it is orbiting.

AXIS (pl. **AXES**) The line around which a body spins.

CENTER OF GRAVITY The point at which all of the mass of an object can be balanced.

ECCENTRIC A noncircular, or oval, orbit.

GRAVITY/GRAVITATIONAL PULL The force of attraction between bodies. The larger an object, the more its gravitational pull on other objects.

MOMENTUM The mass of an object multiplied by its velocity.

ORBIT The path followed by one object as it tracks around another.

PERIGEE The point on an orbit where the orbiting object is as close as it ever comes to the object it is orbiting.

PLANE A flat surface.

SIDEREAL MONTH The average time that the Moon takes to return to the same position against the background of stars.

SUN The star that the planets of the solar system revolve around.

SYNODIC MONTH The complete cycle of phases of the Moon as seen from Earth. It is 29.531 solar days (29 days, 12 hours, 44 minutes, 3 seconds).

TIDE Any kind of regular, or cyclic, change that occurs due to the effect of the gravity of one body on another.

◄ This simple tidal sequence shows how the passage of the Moon causes the movement of the tides. In turn, the tides act as a frictional brake on the rotation of the Earth, causing the Earth and Moon to move apart slowly.

In practice, such things as the complicated shape of the ocean basins cause the high and low tides to sweep around the edge of the ocean basins.

The importance of gravity

There are two high TIDES (and therefore two low tides) each day on Earth. One high and one low tide are caused by the GRAVITATIONAL PULL of the Moon and to a lesser extent by the Sun, and the other high and low tide by the way the Earth and Moon together orbit the Sun.

As the Earth-Moon system orbits the Sun, CENTRIFUGAL FORCE tends to throw everything in the direction away from the Sun, causing, for example, a high tide away from the Sun. Although they have quite different causes, the two high tides occur exactly at the same time on the opposing sides of the Earth.

The Earth spins around the Sun so fast that if it were not for the Earth's GRAVITY, the ocean waters would all flow to the side of the Earth that is facing away from the Sun and fly off into space.

Although the Earth's gravity holds the ocean waters to the surface, the spinning effect of the Earth is powerful enough to ensure that there is always a high tide on the side of the Earth facing away from the Sun.

The interaction of the Moon and the Earth acts like a drag on the Earth through the Moon's effect on the tides.

The Moon is not the only body to have an influence on the Earth's tides. Even though the Sun is much farther away, its GRAVITATIONAL FIELD is far stronger. Its effect is about half that of the Moon's and acts in a different cycle. Even other planets feel the Sun's gravity.

The combined cycles help produce the pattern of the tides. When they act together, they reinforce each other to cause a high-ranging or SPRING TIDE (maximum height difference from high to low tide) or a low-ranging NEAP TIDE (minimum height difference from high to low tide).

The seasons

The Earth moves in two ways—it tilts as it spins, and it travels around the Sun. These two movements produce the SEASONS—spring, summer, fall, and winter—for people who live away from the EQUATOR.

Northern summer

The key to the seasons is the way the Earth is tilted at 23.5°. This tilt causes one part of the Earth to face more directly into the sunlight. In this part it is summer, while in the other part it is winter.

The effect is more pronounced at higher **LATITUDES** and is less obvious in the tropics.

Although the Earth has clear seasons because its axis is tilted to the plane of its orbit, the Moon is almost upright (normal) in its orbit. As a result, it has no seasons. Sunlight is but glancing light at the poles on the Moon, and they are always almost dark and cold.

CENTRIFUGAL FORCE A force that acts on an orbiting or spinning body, tending to oppose gravity and move away from the center of rotation.

EQUATOR The ring drawn around a body midway between the poles.

GRAVITATIONAL FIELD The region surrounding a body in which that body's gravitational force can be felt.

GRAVITY The force of attraction between bodies. The larger an object, the more its gravitational pull on other objects.

LATITUDE Angular distance north or south of the equator, measured through 90°.

NEAP TIDE A tide showing the smallest difference between high and low tides.

SEASONS The characteristic cycle of events in the heating of the Earth that causes related changes in weather patterns.

SPRING TIDE A tide showing the greatest difference between high and low tides.

Northern spring

Northern winter

Northern autumn

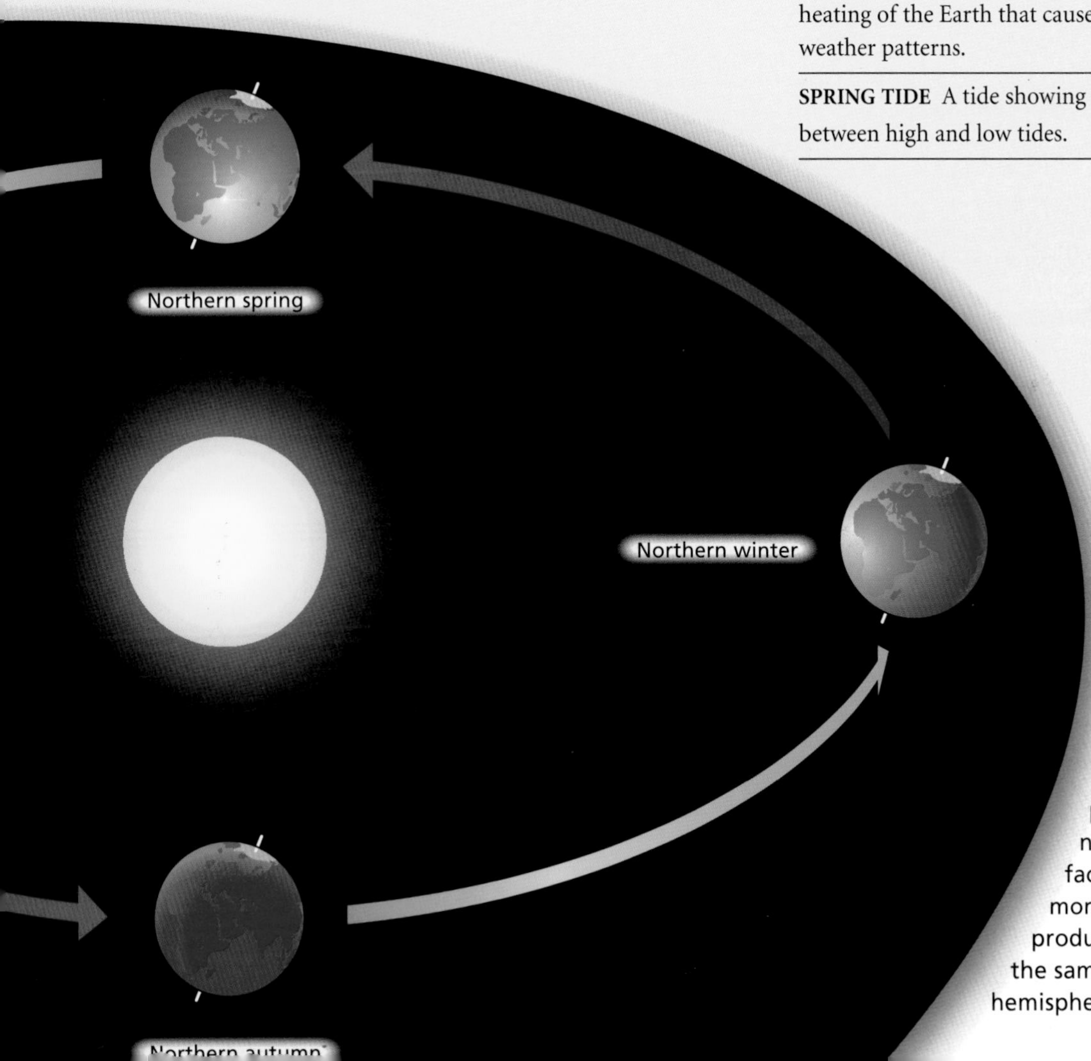

◄ This picture shows how the tilted Earth moves around the Sun. Because the tilt is always in the same direction, for one part of the year the northern hemisphere faces toward the Sun more directly. That produces summer. At the same time, the other hemisphere has winter.

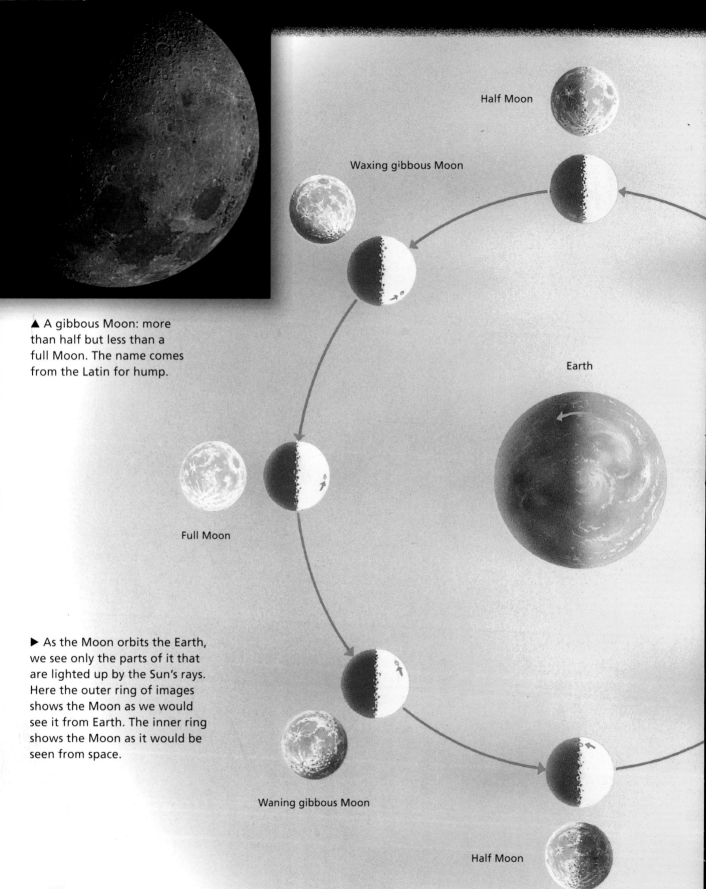

Half Moon

Waxing gibbous Moon

▲ A gibbous Moon: more
than half but less than a
full Moon. The name comes
from the Latin for hump.

Earth

Full Moon

▶ As the Moon orbits the Earth,
we see only the parts of it that
are lighted up by the Sun's rays.
Here the outer ring of images
shows the Moon as we would
see it from Earth. The inner ring
shows the Moon as it would be
seen from space.

Waning gibbous Moon

Half Moon

The phases of the Moon

Although the Earth and the Moon have no light of their own, they are illuminated by the Sun. Because the Moon can lie between the Earth and the Sun, it exhibits **PHASES**—changes in the way it looks.

The phases begin with a new Moon, go through a waxing (increasing) **CRESCENT** Moon, a half Moon, and a waxing **GIBBOUS** Moon to a full Moon. The phases continue as a waning (decreasing) gibbous Moon, a half Moon, and a waning crescent Moon, finishing with darkness, or a new Moon.

A gibbous Moon occurs when the Moon is between half a full Moon and a full Moon. The crescent Moon is less than half a full Moon.

Waxing crescent Moon

New Moon

Waning crescent Moon

CRESCENT The appearance of the Moon when it is between a new Moon and a half Moon.

GIBBOUS When between half and a full disk of a body can be seen lighted by the Sun.

PHASE The differing appearance of a body that is closer to the Sun, and that is illuminated by it.

▼ A crescent Moon: less than a half Moon.

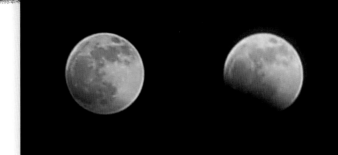

▶ The stages of a lunar eclipse.

ANNULAR Ringlike.

APOGEE The point on an orbit where the orbiting object is at its farthest from the object it is orbiting.

CORONA (pl. **CORONAE**) A colored circle seen around a bright object such as a star.

ECLIPSE The time when light is cut off by a body coming between the observer and the source of the illumination (for example, eclipse of the Sun), or when the body the observer is on comes between the source of illumination and another body (for example, eclipse of the Moon).

LUNAR Anything to do with the Moon.

PENUMBRA A region that is in semidarkness during an eclipse.

PERIGEE The point on an orbit where the orbiting object is as close as it ever comes to the object it is orbiting.

SAROS CYCLE The interval of 18 years $11^{1}/_{3}$ days needed for the Earth, Sun, and Moon to come back into the same relative positions. It controls the pattern of eclipses.

SOLAR Anything to do with the Sun.

TOTAL ECLIPSE When one body (such as the Moon or Earth) completely obscures the light source from another body (such as the Earth or Moon).

UMBRA A region that is in complete darkness during an eclipse.

Eclipses

An **ECLIPSE** occurs when three bodies happen to line up, and one body blocks out the light from another. But the Moon is barely big enough to block out the Sun (and cause a **TOTAL ECLIPSE**) when it is at its closest (**PERIGEE**). When the Earth is farthest from the Moon (**APOGEE**), a total eclipse does not occur. Part of the Sun is always visible as the Moon moves between the Sun and the Earth. This is called an **ANNULAR** eclipse.

Both **SOLAR** and **LUNAR** eclipses occur in groups separated by about 18.6 years. This interval is called the **SAROS CYCLE**.

▼ During a solar eclipse the Moon prevents any light from reaching a small area of the Earth's surface called the **UMBRA**. Beyond this spot a large part of the Sun is obscured, and people see a partial eclipse. This larger area is called a **PENUMBRA**.

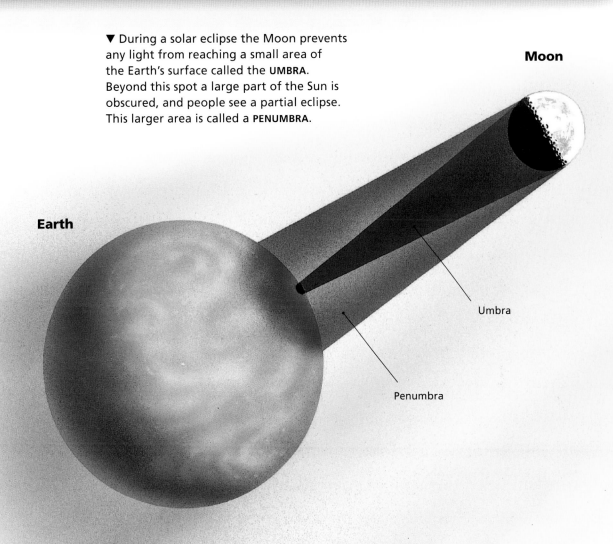

Moon

Earth

Umbra

Penumbra

◀ This picture shows a so-called "diamond ring," the effect seen immediately after a solar eclipse, when the first rays of the Sun appear like a diamond jewel against the ring of the Sun's **CORONA**.

2: PLANET EARTH

The Earth lies beyond Mercury and Venus, and is the third-closest planet to the Sun.

When we look at the other planets, we see them as strange; but in fact, the Earth is, seen from any of the other planets, far stranger. That is because the Earth is the only planet where water can exist in all three forms—liquid, solid, and gas—all at the same time. And, above all, it is strange because it has on its surface carbon-based life forms (living things like us and plants) that, as far as we know, are unique.

The Earth in the solar system

The Earth lies about 149,573,000 km from the Sun. It speeds around its **ORBIT** at nearly 30 km a second, taking 365.2 Earth days to make a complete revolution around the Sun. The Earth also spins on its tilted **AXIS**, revolving once every 23 hours, 56 minutes, and 4 seconds.

If you were to organize the planets in the **SOLAR SYSTEM**, you would find that the Earth is the fifth largest. But it is still a mere speck compared to Jupiter and the other giants of the solar system. It is one of the small rocky planets that mostly lie close to the Sun.

APOLLO The program developed in the United States by NASA to get people to the Moon's surface and back safely.

AXIS (pl. **AXES**) The line around which a body spins.

ORBIT The path followed by one object as it tracks around another.

SOLAR SYSTEM The Sun and the bodies orbiting around it.

▶ Humans first saw the Earth as a globe through the cameras of the **APOLLO** 8 mission to the Moon in December 1968. This is one of the most famous pictures from that eventful mission.
(For other Apollo pictures see pages 44–57.)

For more on the Apollo missions see Volume 6: *Journey into space.*

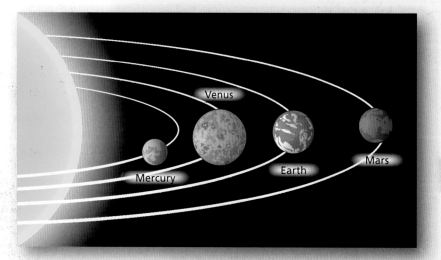

◀ The Earth is the third rocky planet from the Sun.

Details of the other rocky bodies can be found in Volume 4: *Rocky planets.*

◄ Multiple views of the Earth as it rotates about its axis. The South Pole and Antarctic are near the bottom of the picture. The top of the picture is at about latitude 35°N.

The Earth orbits the Sun on a more circular path than most of the other planets. When looked at from above the North Pole, the Earth revolves counterclockwise. That is the same direction as the Sun is revolving.

The Earth has a single **SATELLITE** that we call the Moon. The Moon is large compared to the Earth, and much larger relative to its parent planet than the moons of other planets are. Some people therefore regard the Earth and Moon as a double planet system.

The Earth's gravity

Every object in the universe has a **GRAVITATIONAL FIELD**. The size of the field varies with the **MASS** of the object. The Earth's **GRAVITY** is much larger than that of the Moon, and it is this gravitational field that keeps the Moon orbiting the Earth in just the same way as all of the satellites do that we have recently put into space.

The gravitational field of the Earth causes **TIDES** to develop on the Moon. The line of greatest attraction by the Earth sweeps through the Moon as the Moon spins. That does, in fact, make the Moon change shape continually (bulge toward the Earth) by a small amount as it spins. The Moon, in turn, generates smaller but significant tides in the body of the Earth and in the water and air on the surface. The most important and noticeable result of this is to cause the Earth's surface waters to flow toward the Moon and so create ocean tides (as shown on page 9).

The Earth's size and shape

The Earth has a **RADIUS** of 6,378 km (it is 12,756 km across) at the equator and a **CIRCUMFERENCE** of 40,076 km. Because of the rapid spinning of the Earth **CENTRIFUGAL FORCES** make the Earth bulge at the equator, and so the Earth is not a true **SPHERE**. It is correspondingly flattened at the poles, where the radius is 6,371 km (it is 12,742 km across).

The area of the Earth's surface is 509,600,000 square km, of which 71% is ocean.

If you could weigh the Earth, it would have a mass of $6 \times 1,021$ metric tonnes. Its density is, on average, $5.517\,g/cm^3$ (although this average masks great differences between the very dense core and the much less dense crust).

The Earth's magnetic field

The Earth has a powerful **MAGNETIC FIELD** produced by the churning movements of its **MOLTEN** iron **CORE**. This magnetic field reaches far above the surface (see pages 20–21). That is a hugely important property because it traps **ELECTRONS**, **PROTONS**, and other fast-moving particles, which could kill all living things if they reached the surface. The trapped particles form **RADIATION** belts around the Earth called the Van Allen radiation belts. It is these belts that are responsible for lighting effects over the poles called auroras (see pages 20–21).

CENTRIFUGAL FORCE A force that acts on an orbiting or spinning body, tending to oppose gravity and move away from the center of rotation.

CIRCUMFERENCE The distance around the edge of a circle or sphere.

CORE The central region of a body.

ELECTRONS Negatively charged particles that are parts of atoms.

GRAVITATIONAL FIELD The region surrounding a body in which that body's gravitational force can be felt.

GRAVITY The force of attraction between bodies.

MAGNETIC FIELD The region of influence of a magnetic body.

MASS The amount of matter in an object.

MOLTEN Liquid, suggesting that it has changed from a solid.

PROTONS Positively charged particles from the core of an atom.

RADIATION The transfer of energy in the form of waves (such as light and heat) or particles (such as from radioactive decay of a material).

RADIUS (pl. **RADII**) The distance from the center to the outside of a circle or sphere.

SATELLITE An object that is in an orbit around another object, usually a planet.

SPHERE A ball-shaped object.

TIDE Any kind of regular, or cyclic, change that occurs due to the effect of the gravity of one body on another.

◄ Here is the Earth seen with the Moon in about their correct proportions, the Earth being four times the diameter of the Moon. The gas giant Saturn and its rings, which combined are 21 times the diameter of the Earth, would fit inside the gap between the Earth and the Moon.

The magnetosphere and the auroras

The **MAGNETOSPHERE** is a giant invisible shell beyond the Earth's **ATMOSPHERE**. It reaches about ten Earth diameters in front of the Earth and several thousand Earth diameters back into space, forming a tail.

The magnetosphere does not contain any air from the Earth, but it is where the **MAGNETISM** from the Earth reaches out into the **SOLAR WIND** (the flow of charged particles from the Sun). The power produced in this region is about 100 billion watts, and part of that power produces the nighttime displays called **AURORAS**.

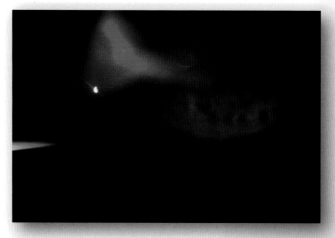

▲▶ Two forms of aurora seen from space.

▼ This cross section shows the way the magnetosphere is buffeted by the solar wind. The result is to squash the magnetosphere in the direction of the solar wind and to produce a long tail in the "lee" of the Earth.

Solar wind

The magnetotail is the portion of a planetary magnetosphere that is pushed in the direction of the solar wind.

An aurora is a glow in the **IONOSPHERE** of a planet caused by the interaction between the planet's **MAGNETIC FIELD** and the solar wind.

In the highest **LATITUDES** of the northern hemisphere on Earth the aurora is called the Aurora Borealis, or the Northern Lights; the Aurora Australis, or Southern Lights, is a similar effect in the Earth's southern hemisphere.

The size of the auroras varies with the amount of solar activity. When the activity is intense, the auroras can be seen from latitudes greater than 40°; but during periods of less activity they may only be visible at above 60°.

Auroras are often green, white, red, or blue. They can look like shining curtains, arcs and bands, or patches that continually move and change shape.

ATMOSPHERE The envelope of gases that surrounds the Earth and other bodies in the universe.

AURORA A region of illumination, often in the form of a wavy curtain, high in the atmosphere of a planet.

IONOSPHERE A part of the Earth's atmosphere in which the number of ions (electrically charged particles) is enough to affect how radio waves move.

LATITUDE Angular distance north or south of the equator, measured through 90°.

MAGNETIC FIELD The region of influence of a magnetic body.

MAGNETISM An invisible force that has the property of attracting iron and similar metals.

MAGNETOSPHERE A region in the upper atmosphere, or around a planet, where magnetic phenomena such as auroras are found.

SOLAR WIND The flow of tiny charged particles (called plasma) outward from the Sun.

The atmosphere

The Earth's **ATMOSPHERE** is a mixture of nitrogen (78%) and oxygen (21%), with argon, **WATER VAPOR**, and carbon dioxide making up most of the rest. Notice that hydrogen and helium are both almost absent.

The shells of gases that envelop the Earth are more dense than on some planets (for example, Mars) but far less dense than on others (for example, Jupiter). But the most extraordinary thing about them is that they contain water in all of its states: solid, liquid, and gas. Furthermore, the gases are largely transparent to sunlight (although an **OZONE** layer blocks harmful **ULTRAVIOLET RADIATION**). So the heat energy in sunlight is not absorbed by the air but instead goes directly through it to heat the surface, both land and water.

▶ The atmosphere is the envelope around the Earth that still contains a significant amount of gas. Only the lowest layer, the troposphere, has enough oxygen to support life.

Exosphere (above 600 km from the Earth's surface). Air molecules are very rare at these levels, and helium is the most common gas.

Thermosphere (about 500 km thick). Extremely thin air. Readily absorbs ultraviolet radiation. Within this layer is the ionosphere, the place that bounces back medium (MW) and short (SW) **RADIO WAVES**, allowing them to travel large distances around the world.

Mesosphere (about 50 km thick). Transparent to the Sun's rays. Temperature decreases with height.

Stratosphere (about 30 km thick). The air is very "thin" but contains important ozone gas. Temperature increases with height.

Troposphere (10–12 km thick—thickest over the equator, thinnest at the poles). The layer that contains the clouds. It is mainly transparent to the Sun's rays. The temperature decreases with height.

The lower atmosphere

The heated ground shares its warmth with the air by CONDUCTION, making the lowest layers of the air generally warmer than those above. That is a very unstable situation. Just as when water is heated in a saucepan, the heated gas in the air becomes less dense than the air above it, and so it begins to rise through the more dense air. In turn, the denser air sinks. In this way a circulation is set in train that carries moist air from the surface to areas higher in the atmosphere. This is a process called CONVECTION.

Although the rising air is still warmer than its surroundings as it rises, it nonetheless cools as it moves away from its source of heating. The amount of water that air can carry as vapor gets smaller as the air gets cooler. So, as the air rises, some water vapor begins to CONDENSE, changing to small droplets of liquid water. That is the origin of the Earth's liquid water clouds, and they are quite unique in the solar system.

Eventually the droplets gather and form larger drops (or snowflakes), which are then heavy enough to fall against the draft of rising air. They produce rain or snow. This once more begins the cycle of events that carries water and ice to the land, where it can erode the rocks—again, a unique feature of the solar system (see pages 28–29).

ATMOSPHERE The envelope of gases that surrounds the Earth and other bodies in the universe.

CONDENSE To change state from a gas or vapor to a liquid.

CONDUCTION The transfer of heat between two objects when they touch.

CONVECTION The circulating flow in a fluid (liquid or gas) that occurs when it is heated from below.

LIMB The outer edge of a celestial body, including an atmosphere if it has one.

OZONE A form of oxygen (O_3) with three atoms in each molecule instead of the more usual two (O_2).

RADIATION The transfer of energy in the form of waves (such as light and heat) or particles (such as from radioactive decay of a material).

RADIO WAVES A form of electromagnetic radiation, like light and heat. Radio waves have a longer wavelength than light waves.

ULTRAVIOLET A form of radiation that is just beyond the violet end of the visible spectrum and so is called "ultra" (more than) violet. At the other end of the visible spectrum is "infra" (less than) red.

WATER VAPOR The gaseous form of water. Also sometimes referred to as moisture.

The upper atmosphere

At heights of thousands of kilometers the atmosphere gradually merges with the SOLAR WIND.

Most of the gas MOLECULES in the atmosphere are concentrated in the lowest 10–12 km—a region called the TROPOSPHERE. That is where the clouds form, and the WATER CYCLE operates (see page 29). Above it lies the quieter STRATOSPHERE to an altitude of about 50 kilometers. It is in the stratosphere that ozone molecules absorb ultraviolet rays.

Most of the atmosphere consists of electrically neutral ATOMS and molecules, but at high altitudes more and more particles are electrically charged. This region is called the IONOSPHERE. It extends throughout the MESOSPHERE and THERMOSPHERE but becomes most important above 100 kilometers. Here, because of the greater proportion of charged, or IONIZED, particles, the auroras are generated (see pages 20–21). (*Note:* The radiation belts and magnetic field of the Earth are not related to the belts of the atmosphere, with the Van Allen belts being doughnut-shaped radiation zones that begin 1,000 km above the Earth's surface. The magnetosphere goes through the entire atmosphere and beyond.)

▲ This picture shows the Earth's limb (the edge of the atmosphere). It is highlighted by this view where the Moon is seen through the outer atmosphere. Notice how the thinner upper atmosphere is shown by the clarity of the Moon.

ATOM The smallest particle of an element.

IONIZED Matter that has been converted into small charged particles called ions.

IONOSPHERE A part of the Earth's atmosphere in which the number of ions (electrically charged particles) is enough to affect how radio waves move.

MESOSPHERE One of the upper regions of the atmosphere, beginning at the top of the stratosphere and continuing from 50 km upward until the temperature stops declining.

MOLECULE A group of two or more atoms held together by chemical bonds.

SOLAR WIND The flow of tiny charged particles (called plasma) outward from the Sun.

STRATOSPHERE The region immediately above the troposphere where the temperature increases with height, and the air is always stable.

THERMOSPHERE A region of the upper atmosphere above the mesosphere.

TROPOSPHERE The lowest region of the atmosphere, where all of the Earth's clouds form.

WATER CYCLE The continuous cycling of water, as vapor, liquid, and solid, between the oceans, the atmosphere, and the land.

▲ Storms dominate large parts of the Earth's surface. Reflection from the clouds is what makes it look bright from space. This picture shows a midlatitude CYCLONE.

▲ One of the most powerful features of the atmosphere: a hurricane.

How the atmosphere circulates

Unlike many other planets with an atmosphere, the Earth has significant air flow between the equator and poles. Because it is colder at the poles than at the equator, there is a tendency for warm air to flow to the poles and for cold air to flow to the equator. As this air moves from one LATITUDE to another, it is caught by the changing speed of the Earth and is made to develop into spinning circulations. They are the midlatitude storms, of which the most powerful are HURRICANES.

Changes through time

Another important characteristic of the Earth's atmosphere is that it has changed in composition through time. The primary feature responsible for this has been the development of life on Earth.

The early Earth's atmosphere had little oxygen. But as simple plant life forms developed, they were able to make use of sunlight and the carbon dioxide in the air to build their tissues. As part of this process, they released free oxygen. This process is called **PHOTOSYNTHESIS**, and it began to change the whole of the Earth's atmosphere.

As long as there is enough plant life, free oxygen will remain part of the atmosphere. However, the oxygen is very **REACTIVE** and quite unstable in the large amounts we currently find. Without life it would soon be locked up in **COMPOUNDS** again. It does not occur in such high proportions on any other planet.

The oceans have also changed through the history of the planet. At first, water was spewed out of volcanoes. But at this early time the Sun was not as bright as it is today, and so it would not have heated the Earth as much as it now does. Temperatures on the surface would not normally have been high enough to keep the water from freezing.

However, out of the volcanoes also came carbon dioxide, which trapped heat in the air, making the surface warmer than it otherwise would have been.

But plants removed much of this carbon dioxide at a later date, thus keeping the atmospheric warming from getting out of control in the way that it has on Venus.

COMPOUND A substance made from two or more elements that have chemically combined.

CYCLONE A large storm in which the atmosphere spirals inward and upward.

HURRICANE A very violent cyclone that begins close to the equator, and that contains winds of over 117 km/hr.

LATITUDE Angular distance north or south of the equator, measured through 90°.

PHOTOSYNTHESIS The process that plants use to combine the substances in the environment, such as carbon dioxide, minerals, and water, with oxygen and energy-rich organic compounds by using the energy of sunlight.

PLANKTON Microscopic creatures that float in water.

REACTIVE The ability of a chemical substance to combine readily with other substances. Oxygen is an example of a reactive substance.

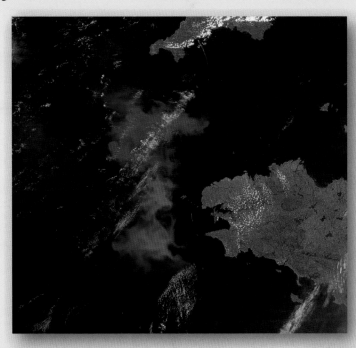

▶ This is a bloom, or rapid growth, of **PLANKTON** in the Atlantic Ocean. It was the development of such primitive life in the oceans that changed the balance of gases in the air, increasing the amount of oxygen, while reducing the amount of carbon dioxide.

Water on the Earth

Although we may swim in warm surface ocean waters, most of the ocean is cold. In fact, the average temperature of the world's oceans is 4°C, which also happens to be the temperature at which water is most dense. The temperature is not far above freezing point, so we barely avoid being a frozen world.

As described in the atmosphere section (pages 22–27), the Earth's water exists as solid, liquid, and gas. Almost all of it is liquid water in the oceans, with small amounts locked up as ice caps and ice sheets, and a tiny gaseous proportion circulating between oceans, atmosphere, and land.

The **WATER CYCLE** (page 29) stretches both into the air and into the rocks. Circulating **WATER VAPOR** reaches up to the top of the **TROPOSPHERE** at 15 km and also **PERCOLATES** 5 km down into rocks.

The water cycle is powered by sunlight. About a third of the Sun's energy that reaches us is used up fueling the water cycle.

CONDENSATION The change of state from a gas or vapor to a liquid.

CONVECTION The circulating flow in a fluid (liquid or gas) that occurs when it is heated from below.

EVAPORATION The change in state from liquid to a gas.

LAVA Hot, melted rock from a volcano. Lava flows onto the surface of a planet and cools and hardens to form new rock.

PERCOLATE To flow by gravity between particles, for example, of soil.

SEDIMENTARY Rocks deposited in layers.

SOLAR RADIATION The light and heat energy sent into space from the Sun.

TROPOSPHERE The lowest region of the atmosphere, where all of the Earth's clouds form.

WATER CYCLE The continuous cycling of water, as vapor, liquid, and solid, between the oceans, the atmosphere, and the land.

WATER VAPOR The gaseous form of water. Also sometimes referred to as moisture.

▼ Because water can occur as ice as well as liquid and gas, it can evaporate from the oceans, make clouds, fall as snow, and be compacted into ice. Ice is one of the most powerful of all eroding agents, as seen here at the Malaspina Glacier, Alaska.

The water cycle

The water cycle is unique to the Earth. Because water can exist as liquid and vapor in the range of Earth temperatures, **EVAPORATION** and **CONDENSATION** are common events. They are not common elsewhere in the solar system.

Precipitation occurs when the water droplets or snowflakes are big enough to fall against the updrafts that produce the cloud.

Water is stored in the clouds in the form of water droplets. These droplets also reflect **SOLAR RADIATION** back to space.

The unique role of plants on planet Earth is shown in part by the way they influence natural cycles. In this case plants take in water through their roots and transpire it back to the air.

Water turns into gas by evaporation. It then rises due to either heating (a process called **CONVECTION**) or global winds. Condensation occurs at higher levels to produce clouds.

As water flows as rivers, the energy of the moving water can cause erosion and thus alter the shape of the planet's surface (see page 40). Chemical reactions can also occur, so that rocks are dissolved away as part of the water cycle.

The majority of the water on the Earth is in the form of liquid water in the oceans. Solar radiation provides the energy to turn a small part of it into gas to produce water vapor in the air.

The Earth has unique rocks because of the rock cycle (see pages 40–41). Although rocks on other planets are impermeable **LAVAS**, many rocks on the Earth are **SEDIMENTARY**. They make up the majority of the water-bearing rocks on Earth. Water is stored in these rocks and slowly transferred to rivers.

The Earth's crust

The earliest Earth collected as a mass of dust and gas that collapsed under the force of **GRAVITY**. That caused a release of heat that made the planet's rocks melt (1). It took a billion years for the surface to cool into a hard crust (2). The early Earth was also bombarded by **METEORITES**. In time **VOLCANOES** developed, and then an atmosphere and oceans (3). Life probably arose in the hot liquids near volcanic eruptions. Slowly the emerging plant life helped absorb carbon dioxide and release oxygen, allowing life to colonize the land and for the present atmosphere to form (4).

Plates

The Earth's "crust" is a general term for its upper, rigid rocks. Scientists call it the **LITHOSPHERE**.

But the crust is not, as it is on many other planets, a continuous shell of similar material. On the Earth the crust is broken into about a dozen large pieces, which have come to be called **PLATES**. Cracking in the plates is the result of movements of materials in the **MANTLE** below the crust. Again, as far as we know, this is a unique feature of our planet.

▲▼ The early history of the crust. Numbers are explained in the text.

ASTHENOSPHERE The region below the lithosphere, and therefore part of the upper mantle, in which some material may be molten.

GRAVITY The force of attraction between bodies.

LITHOSPHERE The upper part of the Earth, corresponding generally to the crust and believed to be about 80 km thick.

MANTLE The region of a planet between the core and the crust.

METEORITE A meteor that reaches the Earth's surface.

PLATE A very large unbroken part of the crust of a planet. Also called tectonic plate.

VOLCANO A mound or mountain that is formed from ash or lava.

▲ An exaggerated view of the location of the plate boundaries on the Earth.

▼ The main layers of the Earth. The diagram is not to scale.

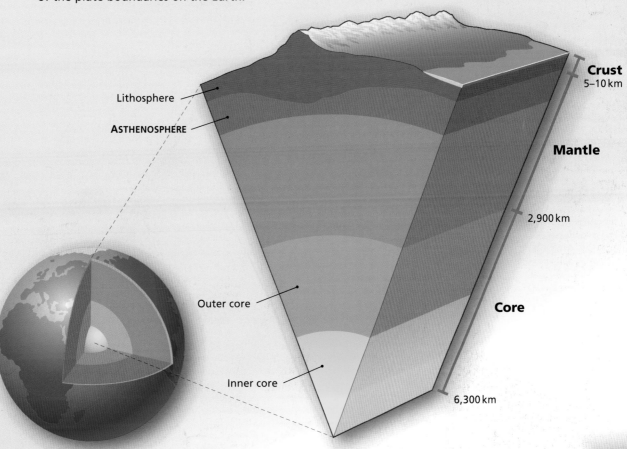

Lithosphere

ASTHENOSPHERE

Crust
5–10 km

Mantle

2,900 km

Outer core

Core

Inner core

6,300 km

Just as **CONVECTION** of air powers the water cycle in the atmosphere, so convection currents power the very slow **PLASTIC** flow of rocks below the surface. In this case the energy comes from the heat flowing up from the center of the Earth and also from **RADIOACTIVE DECAY** of **MINERALS** within the rocks themselves.

Heat rises in some places. As it does so, it melts some rocks, which then flow upward. In some places, such as at the edges of plates, the liquid material, known as **MAGMA**, reaches the surface. We called it **ASH** or **LAVA** depending on whether it solidifies as it is blown into the atmosphere or whether it flows from volcanoes.

To balance the rising material, rock also sinks back into the Earth in other places. That happens along long lines at the edges of plates. They are called **SUBDUCTION ZONES**, and they are marked by more volcanoes and also by extensive **EARTHQUAKES**. The earthquakes are caused as the crust moves in periodic jerks while it reenters the Earth.

ASH Fragments of lava that have cooled and solidified between when they leave a volcano and when they fall to the surface.

CONVECTION The circulating flow in a fluid (liquid or gas) that occurs when it is heated from below.

EARTHQUAKE The shock waves produced by the sudden movement of two pieces of brittle crust.

LAVA Hot, melted rock from a volcano.

MAGMA Hot, melted rock inside the Earth that, when cooled, forms igneous rock.

MINERAL A solid crystalline substance.

PLASTIC The ability of certain solid substances to be molded or deformed to a new shape under pressure without cracking.

RADIOACTIVE DECAY The change that takes place inside radioactive materials and causes them to give out progressively less radiation over time.

SUBDUCTION ZONES Long, relatively thin, but very deep regions of the crust where one plate moves down and under, or subducts, another. They are the source of mountain ranges.

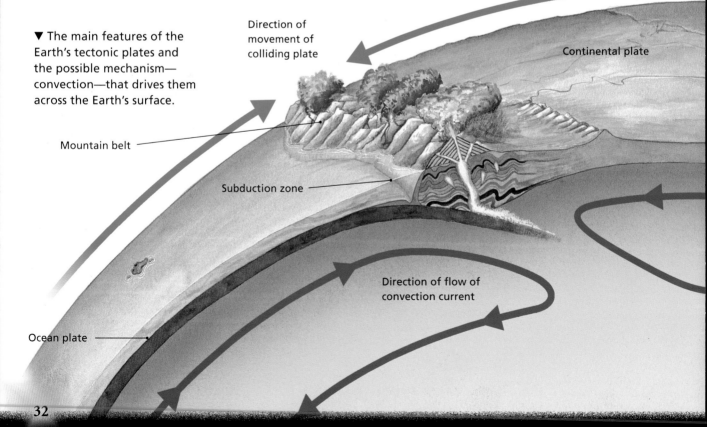

▼ The main features of the Earth's tectonic plates and the possible mechanism—convection—that drives them across the Earth's surface.

Direction of movement of colliding plate

Continental plate

Mountain belt

Subduction zone

Direction of flow of convection current

Ocean plate

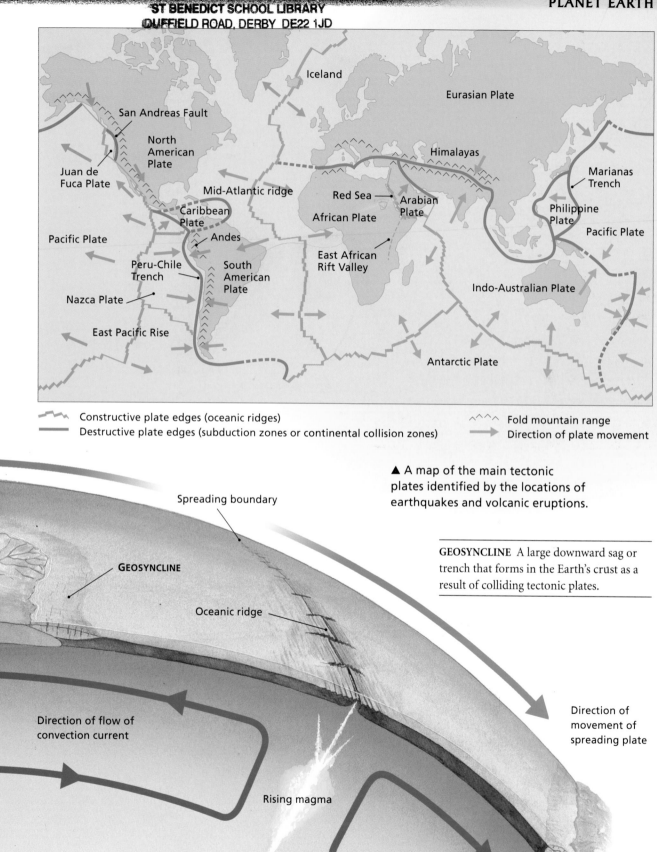

Constructive plate edges (oceanic ridges)
Destructive plate edges (subduction zones or continental collision zones)
Fold mountain range
Direction of plate movement

▲ A map of the main tectonic plates identified by the locations of earthquakes and volcanic eruptions.

GEOSYNCLINE A large downward sag or trench that forms in the Earth's crust as a result of colliding tectonic plates.

Spreading boundary

GEOSYNCLINE

Oceanic ridge

Direction of flow of convection current

Rising magma

Direction of movement of spreading plate

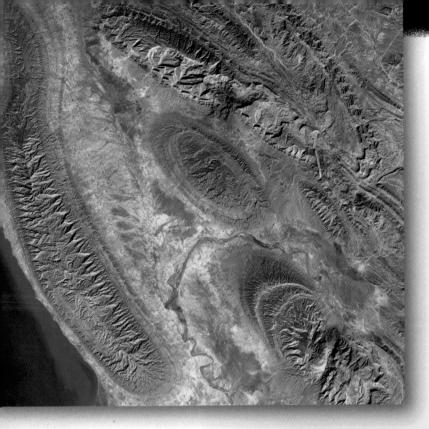

ANTICLINE An arching fold of rock layers where the rocks slope down from the crest.

ASTHENOSPHERE The region below the lithosphere, and therefore part of the upper mantle, in which some material may be molten.

MOUNTAIN RANGE A long, narrow region of very high land that contains several or many mountains.

SEDIMENT Any particles of material that settle out, usually in layers, from a moving fluid such as air or water.

SPACE SHUTTLE NASA's reusable space vehicle that is launched like a rocket but returns like a glider.

▲ When deeply buried rocks are squashed together, such as at subduction zones, they can be folded without breaking. Later, when they are brought to the surface as mountains and then eroded, the pattern of folds is clear to see. This is part of the Zagros Mountains of Iran, showing unroofed **ANTICLINES**.

▼ A cross section through the Alps of Europe gives some idea of the way that the movement of plates crushes rocks into great mountain ranges.

The partially molten layer below the crust is the upper mantle. Scientists call it the **ASTHENOSPHERE**.

At subduction zones deep trenches develop, which are continually filled with sand, clay, and other materials (**SEDIMENT**) washed in after erosion of the land. This material is not as dense as the rocks of the mantle and so tends to float on the mantle. As it is squashed at the subduction zone, it sometimes refuses to sink back into the mantle. When this occurs, the material remains on the surface, but occupies a narrower and narrower zone. The only way for this to happen is for the material of the zones to buckle up. Buckled up and folded rocks of this kind make **MOUNTAIN RANGES**.

▲ Curving ranges of the Canadian Rockies
as seen from the SPACE SHUTTLE. The arrows
show the crustal movements needed to
produce mountain systems of this kind.
Any pattern of mountain ranges suggests
compression at a plate boundary.

Continental drift

The process of crustal movement has been going on for at least three billion years. Evidence that it happens (geologically speaking) quickly is that there is no rock on the ocean floors older than about 200 million years.

Going back in time before three billion years, we also see a world in which CONVECTION was even more powerful, when the crust was only just solidifying, and when collisions between the Earth and other space bodies were more frequent and more damaging. The development of large PLATES that moved, undisturbed by giant impacts from space, had to wait for nearly a billion years of the Earth's development.

When it did happen, it reorganized the distribution of land and sea, of mountains and plains, of desert and tropical areas and cold poles time and time again. The maps on this page show what has happened over just the last 300 million years.

▼ The Earth as it looked in Carboniferous times, 300 million years ago. Notice that most of the continents are gathered around the South Pole, and that they are all joined in a supercontinent called Pangea.

CONVECTION The circulating flow in a fluid (liquid or gas) that occurs when it is heated from below.

PLATE A very large unbroken part of the crust of a planet. Also called tectonic plate.

Key to diagrams

 Ancient landmass

 Modern landmass

 Subduction zone (triangles point in direction of subduction)

 Seafloor spreading ridge

▼▶ The Earth's surface has been on the move ever since the crust formed. Reconstructions of the past show a very different planet 300 million years ago (below), 190 million years ago (opposite top), and 94 million years ago (opposite bottom). Such differences would have had major effects on the water cycle, the atmosphere, and the formation of mountains.

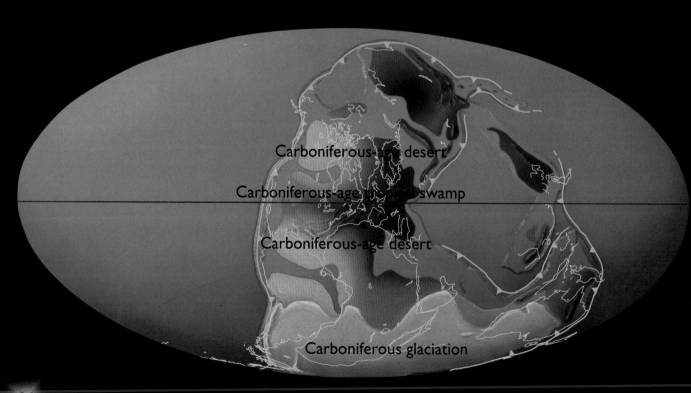

Carboniferous-age desert

Carboniferous-age tropical swamp

Carboniferous-age desert

Carboniferous glaciation

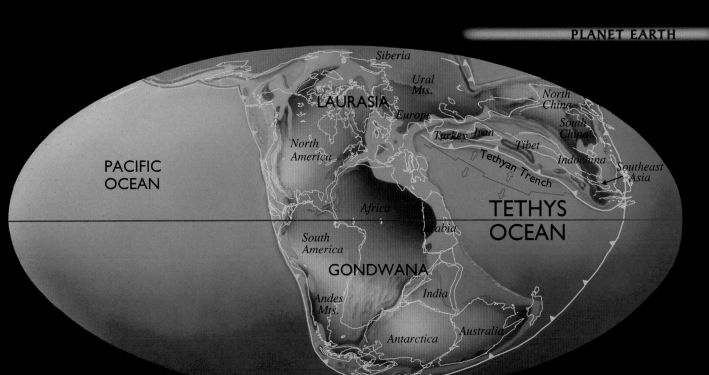

▲ The Earth as it looked in Jurassic times, 190 million years ago. Notice that many of the modern continents are still joined together as a supercontinent called Gondwanaland.

▼ The Earth as it looked in Late Cretaceous times, 94 million years ago. The continents have moved considerably from Jurassic times and have mainly become separated. Australia is still combined with Antarctica; and large parts of modern North America, North Africa, and Europe are underwater. India is still off the coast of southern Africa.

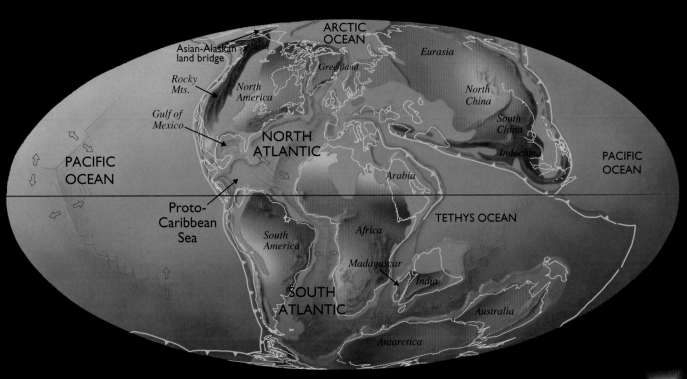

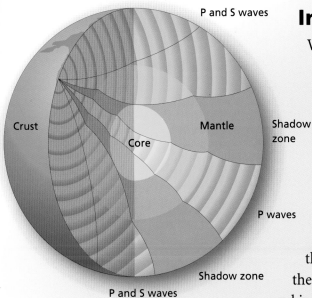

P and S waves

Crust

Mantle

Core

Shadow zone

P waves

Shadow zone

P and S waves

▲ How earthquake waves resonate through the Earth. By studying the patterns of earthquake waves, it is possible to find out the general nature of the structure of the planet.

Inside the Earth

We know more about the structure of the Earth than about any other body in space. That is because we can make direct observations, mainly by monitoring SEISMIC (EARTHQUAKE) waves.

The pattern of earthquake waves suggests that the Earth is made of three zones: a thin surface CRUST (on average 35 km thick, but below mountain ranges and in other places over 200 km thick); a thicker, mainly solid, but also partly PLASTIC MANTLE that extends to 2,900 km below the surface; and a mainly liquid CORE that extends to the center. The outer part of the core is probably liquid and is the source of the Earth's MAGNETIC FIELD. The inner part (up to 1,200 km from the center) is under more pressure and is probably solid.

▼ Features created by volcanic activity are much the same as could be imagined on other planets. It is the erosion of these features, which is vastly different on the Earth compared with other planets, that gives the land surface a quite unique look. Typical erosional features are shown in the diagram.

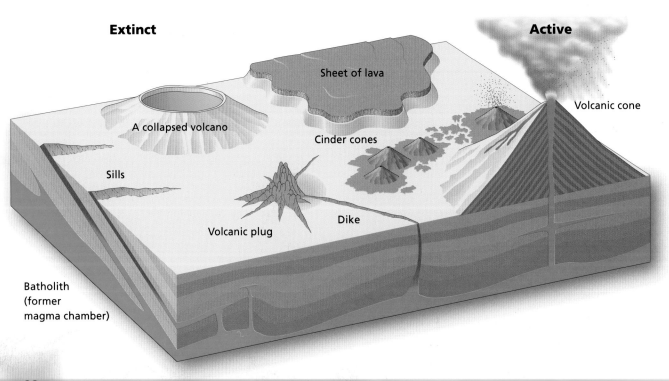

Extinct

Active

Sheet of lava

Volcanic cone

A collapsed volcano

Cinder cones

Sills

Volcanic plug

Dike

Batholith (former magma chamber)

◄ Volcanic eruptions, such as Mt. Etna in the Mediterranean, do not just release ash and lava and build the Earth's crust; they also release large amounts of water as vapor and a range of other gases. Such outpourings created the first atmosphere and still contribute to it.

The whole of the Earth is dominated by just a few chemical elements: iron, oxygen, silicon, and magnesium. Together they account for over nine-tenths of the **MASS** of the planet.

Oxygen is the reactive key **ELEMENT**. By combining with silicon, it makes silicates, such as quartz, and the **MINERALS** in rocks, such as granite. By combining with aluminum as well (a relatively common element in the crust but almost absent elsewhere in the Earth), minerals such as feldspars and soils such as clay are formed.

In the mantle silicates linked with iron make the minerals that form rocks, such as gabbro and basalt. In contrast to the rocks of which the crust and the mantle are formed, the core is probably made of iron, with smaller amounts of oxygen and sulfur.

When we realized that the Earth has a different chemistry in its inner and its outer regions, we could figure out how the other planets emerged.

The difference between surface and core chemistry comes about because of differences in heat and pressure, which both increase toward the center of the Earth.

Interestingly, the core of the Earth, at 7,500°C, is hotter than the surface of the Sun. This heat, together with warmth produced as **RADIOACTIVE** elements decay within the Earth, provides the energy that powers the movement of the **PLATES** and the production of **VOLCANOES**.

CORE The central region of a body.

CRUST The solid outer surface of a rocky body.

EARTHQUAKE The shock waves produced by the sudden movement of two pieces of brittle crust.

ELEMENT A substance that cannot be decomposed into simpler substances by chemical means.

MAGNETIC FIELD The region of influence of a magnetic body.

MANTLE The region of a planet between the core and the crust.

MASS The amount of matter in an object.

MINERAL A solid crystalline substance.

PLASTIC The ability of certain solid substances to be molded or deformed to a new shape under pressure without cracking.

PLATE A very large unbroken part of the crust of a planet. Also called tectonic plate.

RADIOACTIVE The property of some materials that emit radiation or energetic particles from the nucleus of their atoms.

SEISMIC Shaking, relating to earthquakes.

VOLCANO A mound or mountain that is formed from ash or lava.

▼ This picture of the North African coast shows three processes of erosion in action that appear not to occur anywhere else in the solar system. (1) Wind is blowing sand off the Sahara Desert into the Mediterranean Sea. (2) Rivers are bringing sand, silt, and mud to the sea from the land, forming the Nile Delta (the green triangular area). (3) The waves are carrying sand along the coast (the light-colored sea to the right of the Nile Delta). All these processes will rapidly change the shape of the land.

Erosion on the Earth

Erosion, the wearing away of solid rocks and the formation of fine materials such as soils, is a direct result of the WATER CYCLE operating on the land surface.

Although other planets have an almost unchanging surface, the land surface of the Earth is changing constantly, producing a wide variety of types of scenery. The water cycle also provides the water that living things need to survive on land.

The rock cycle

The movement of MAGMA from the mantle to the surface and its erosion by the weather and oceans produce a continually changing surface. This transfer of material did not just happen once but has gone on time after time through the mechanism that transfers eroded material back to the mantle or back to the crust. Together all of these facets of landshaping make the rock cycle.

▼ The Earth's surface is a balance of building and erosion. This is Cotopaxi Volcano, specially colored to show height. Notice that the volcanic cone, which we are looking at from directly above, and which is produced by the buildup of layers, is scarred by deep valleys, the effect of water erosion.

There is much evidence for the rock cycle. We can see volcanoes adding new material to the crust as **ASH** and **LAVA**, and we can see rivers, wind, ice, and waves carrying eroded rock to the oceans, where it is deposited.

The deposited material settles in layers and gradually compresses under the weight of more **SEDIMENT** to make layers of rock. This kind of rock is called **SEDIMENTARY**.

Much of the sediment accumulates around the edges of continents. Since they are also often the boundaries of plates, there is also a mechanism for scraping the sedimentary rocks off the ocean floor and making them into land (see pages 32–34).

Thus, from being deep under the ocean, the rocks eventually find themselves forced up onto the crust, usually as parts of new mountain systems.

Sometimes the fact that rocks are sedimentary is easy to see because they are still in level layers. But more often they have been contorted, so they now make broad arches or dips or even stand on edge.

ASH Fragments of lava that have cooled and solidified between when they leave a volcano and when they fall to the surface.

LAVA Hot, melted rock from a volcano.

MAGMA Hot, melted rock inside the Earth that, when cooled, forms igneous rock.

SEDIMENT Any particles of material that settle out, usually in layers, from a moving fluid such as air or water.

SEDIMENTARY Rocks deposited in layers.

WATER CYCLE The continuous cycling of water, as vapor, liquid, and solid, between the oceans, the atmosphere, and the land.

▼ These Grand Canyon cliffs show a typical staircase of layers that are the signature of sedimentary rock. In this case they have not been buckled. Sedimentary rock of this kind is produced on no other planet.

3: THE MOON

The **MOON** is so close and yet so tantalizingly strange and unknown. Even though we have been there and walked on it, we have done little more than literally scratch the surface of this, our natural **SATELLITE**.

Some things we know about the Moon are obvious enough. The Moon is about 3,500 km across, and it is made of rock. It **ORBITS** around us in a near circle some 384,000 km from the Earth. Each **LUNAR** day lasts for 2 Earth weeks.

The Moon is not a true sphere (ball-shape), nor is the Earth. The Moon is flattened very slightly, although less than the Earth. The longest diameter is in the direction pointing directly to the Earth.

The Moon's gravity

The Moon is small so it cannot have the same **GRAVITY** as the Earth. Gravity on the Moon is about a sixth of that on the Earth.

Astronauts experienced this dramatically. A person weighing 80 kilograms on the Earth would weigh only 13 kilograms on the Moon. As a result, even with heavy space suits, astronauts can easily hop and skip around on the Moon's surface.

CRATER A deep bowl-shaped depression in the surface of a body formed by the high-speed impact of another, smaller body.

GALILEO A U.S. space probe launched in October 1989 and designed for intensive investigation of Jupiter.

GRAVITY The force of attraction between bodies.

LUNAR Anything to do with the Moon.

MOON The natural satellite that orbits the Earth.

ORBIT The path followed by one object as it tracks around another.

SATELLITE An object that is in an orbit around another object, usually a planet.

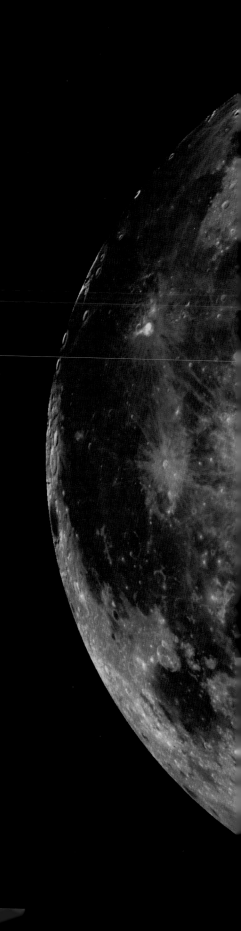

▶ The Moon as seen from the **GALILEO** spacecraft. The distinct bright **CRATER** at the bottom of the image is the Tycho impact basin. The dark areas are lava rock-filled impact basins (mare): Oceanus Procellarum (on the left), Mare Imbrium (center left), Mare Serenitatis and Mare Tranquillitatis (center), and Mare Crisium (near the right edge).

For the mission to the Moon see Volume 6: *Journey into space*.

The Moon's atmosphere

Look at any picture of the Moon showing the view into space, and you will see that the lunar sky is always black. That is because the blue sky we are used to is created by light waves being altered (called **DIFFRACTION**) as they enter our **ATMOSPHERE**. Without a substantial atmosphere that cannot occur, and so the Moon's sky is invisible.

The low gravity of the Moon means that any gases present on the surface tend to float away more readily than they do on the Earth. That is why there is no thick atmosphere encircling the Moon. That does not mean there is no atmosphere at all; but it is extremely thin, and **MOLECULES** in it are so sparse that they rarely collide.

When we make a sound on the Earth, it is carried through the air by molecules colliding with each other. Without collisions of molecules there can be no sound through the air. The Moon is therefore silent. If you were able to speak without a space suit, no sound would come from your mouth.

The main gases naturally present are neon, hydrogen, helium, and argon. Argon is released from lunar rocks by the decay of **RADIOACTIVE** potassium. Neon, hydrogen, and helium come from the **SOLAR WIND** that blows all around the Moon.

The atmosphere is neither thick enough to have any braking effect on anything moving about, nor can it develop winds.

Without the atmosphere and winds that we have, and with no oceans to soak up heat and regulate temperatures, the surface of the Moon reaches over 120°C during the day but drops to −170°C at night.

▲▼▶ The surface of the Moon is covered with many large rocks and also a thin layer of soil almost like dust. You can get a clear idea of the surface from these pictures and the one on pages 48–49.

(Top left) Astronaut Buzz Aldrin steps down to the lunar surface during the **APOLLO** 11 mission. Notice that the lander does not sink into deep soil.

The detail (bottom left) shows a bootprint and the thin layer of dust that covers the Moon's surface.

(Opposite top right) There is no wind on the surface of the Moon because there is so little atmosphere. That is shown by the fact that the flag has to be supported along its top edge.

The Moon's surface

We depend on our thicker atmosphere to protect us from space, and in particular to make most **METEORITES** burn up before they reach the surface. Since the Moon has no such protective shell, meteorites arriving there collide with the surface, creating impact **CRATERS**. They are what we can see so clearly from the Earth. It is these impacts that have shattered meteorites and the Moon surface to produce the "soil" that is now found by astronauts. Every part of the surface has extensive impact craters, some small, some enormously large (see pages 50–51). However, there are remarkable differences between the near side (that faces us) and the far side (that we never see from Earth).

APOLLO The program developed in the United States by NASA to get people to the Moon's surface and back safely.

ATMOSPHERE The envelope of gases that surrounds the Earth and other bodies in the universe.

CRATER A deep bowl-shaped depression in the surface of a body formed by the high-speed impact of another, smaller body.

DIFFRACTION The bending of light as it goes through materials of different density.

METEORITE A meteor that reaches the Earth's surface.

MOLECULE A group of two or more atoms held together by chemical bonds.

RADIOACTIVE The property of some materials that emit radiation or energetic particles from the nucleus of their atoms.

SOLAR WIND The flow of tiny charged particles (called plasma) outward from the Sun.

◄ Near side and far side of the Moon. This image shows parts of both the near side and the far side of the Moon. The near side is to the right, the far side to the left.

The circular Orientale Basin, 1,000 kilometers across, is near the center. At the upper right is the large, dark Oceanus Procellarum; below it is the smaller Mare Humorum.

These features, like the small, dark Mare Orientale in the center of the basin, formed over three billion years ago as lava flowed.

At the lower left, among the southern cratered highlands of the far side, is the South Pole-Aitken Basin, similar to Orientale but twice the diameter and much older and more affected by cratering and weathering.

The cratered highlands of the near and far sides and the maria ("seas") are covered with scattered bright, young **RAY** craters.

Near side of the Moon

A combination of giant impacts and **LAVA** outpourings has formed the largest features on the surface. Known as maria (singular **MARE**, from the Latin meaning "sea"), they are the **BASINS** that can be seen as dark-colored blotches on the Moon. Where lava has not formed, the land stands up as highlands and produces the bright areas that we see.

The main period when impact craters formed was during the early stages of the Moon's formation. As a result, we can use the extent of cratering as a rough guide to the age of some surface features. The maria show the least cratering, suggesting that they are the youngest features. The highlands show many more craters and so are very old.

During the history of the Moon there has been considerable volcanic activity. Thin, runny, lava flooded up from the interior, covering vast areas very quickly. Only in a few places is evidence of more sticky lava found, which tends to make domes in the centers of craters.

▼ This is an angled view of the lunar far side from the Apollo 16 spacecraft. Among other craters the largest, just above center left, is the Leonov Crater.

BASIN A large depression in the ground (bigger than a crater).

LAVA Hot, melted rock from a volcano.

MARE (pl. **MARIA**) A flat, dark plain created by lava flows. They were once thought to be seas.

RAY A line across the surface of a planet or moon made by material from a crater being flung across the surface.

REFLECTIVE To bounce back any light that falls on a surface.

Far side of the Moon

Rather extraordinarily, in contrast to the near side, the far side consists of mainly cratered highlands with very small areas of mare. Lava has not flowed out and covered the crater bottoms on the far side in the same way as it has on the near side. This contrast remains to be explained.

How the Moon reflects light

The Moon appears to shine brightly. But in fact, it is nowhere near as **REFLECTIVE** as the Earth, bouncing back only a small amount of the sunlight that falls on it.

The craters and the great roughness of the ground, in general, have a strange effect on the way the Moon reflects light. When the Moon is full, it reflects light to us 11 times more strongly than when it is at half Moon, even though a difference of only two times would be expected. This is explained by the fact that the Moon's face is covered with deep craters. We suddenly see an increased brightening as full Moon approaches, and light is also reflected from the bottoms of the craters.

This dramatic picture shows the Moon rover vehicle that was used on the Apollo 17 mission. Footprints can be seen in the soil that masks the rocky surface of the Moon.

The large boulder in the foreground is angular, suggesting that it was created by an event that shattered a much larger piece of rock, but that there has been no erosion since. Smaller fragments to the right of the boulder are also angular and unweathered. They may all be the debris created as a result of an earlier meteorite impact.

The soil is very thin, and so the rolling landforms in the background must reflect the shape of the rock below, possibly the result of ancient lava flows.

Craters on the Moon

CRATERS are one of the most extensive features of the Moon's surface. They were made by the impact of METEORITES.

Meteorites can strike the surface of the Moon more forcefully than the surface of the Earth because there is no thick atmosphere to slow them down. They also survive intact because there are no WEATHERING processes on the Moon like those on the Earth (temperature, wind, water, and ice).

As each meteorite strikes the surface, the collision not only throws out huge amounts of material, but very high temperatures are created, which change the nature of many of the rocks.

Thus molten rocks are splattered out of the crater, together with solid material that has shattered rather than melted.

Larger craters are very deep as well as wide. One, Aristarchus, is about 40 kilometers in diameter and 4 kilometers deep.

This ancient impact created a great pit, but at the same time pushed material away so that a tall rim developed. Such rims are tall enough to be called mountains.

CRATER A deep bowl-shaped depression in the surface of a body formed by the high-speed impact of another, smaller body.

GRAVITY The force of attraction between bodies. The larger an object, the more its gravitational pull on other objects.

METEORITE A meteor that reaches the Earth's surface.

RAY A line across the surface of a planet or moon made by material from a crater being flung across the surface.

WEATHERING The breaking down of a rock, perhaps by water, ice, or repeated heating and cooling.

▼ An artist's impression of a meteorite hitting the surface of the Moon and creating a crater, together with the debris that forms rays.

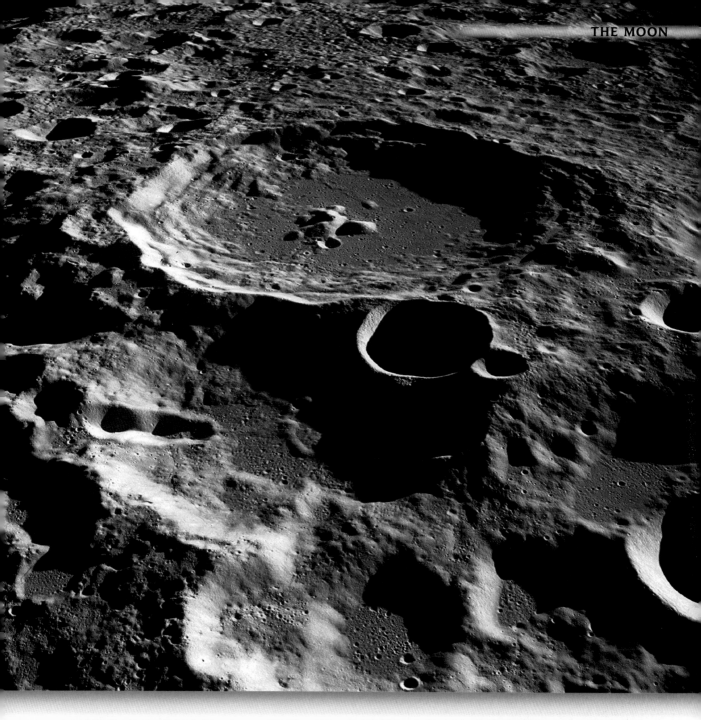

Light-colored **RAYS** around craters are made by ejected material hitting the lunar surface. They lead us to think that craters with rays are much younger than those without.

Over huge periods of time the effects of **GRAVITY** collapse some parts of the rims, producing a stepped, or terracelike edge. At the same time, material thrown from other impact craters gradually obliterates the rays of older craters.

▲ An angled view of the Crater Daedalus on the lunar far side as seen from the Apollo 11 spacecraft in lunar orbit. The view looks southwest. Daedalus has a diameter of about 80 kilometers. This is a typical scene showing the rugged terrain on the far side of the Moon.

Moon soil and Moon rock

As mentioned on page 46, the Moon's surface appears to be made of dark and light rocks. The maria are dark and contain lavas. Their darkness is due to the large amount of iron in the **MINERALS** of the rocks. The brighter highlands are also made of molten rocks, in this case a kind of granite with fine **CRYSTALS**.

Many of the rocks are made of large sharp-edged fragments, which must have been formed by the building up of materials thrown from impact **CRATERS**. The most likely way this could have happened is if a later impact fused together the broken rocks of a previous impact.

The Moon cannot have a true soil because it would have to be a mixture of rocks and living tissue. On the Moon "soils" are mainly dustlike and are the broken-down remains of rocks alone. In this case, with no water to break up the rocks as on the Earth, fragments have been produced during impacts by tiny **METEORITES**. One result of rocks breaking by impact is a large proportion of glassy particles in the "soil."

The skin of Moon rocks and soil has one strange property: It contains fragments of the Sun. That is because the particles of the Sun in the **SOLAR WIND** are not trapped in the atmosphere as they are on the Earth, but reach the ground at high speed and embed themselves in the surface materials.

▶ These orange glass spheres and fragments are the finest particles ever brought back from the Moon. They range in size from 20 to 45 **MICRONS** and are about the same size as the particles that make up **SILT** on Earth.

The orange particles, which are intermixed with black and black-speckled grains, come from the Taurus-Littrow landing site investigated by the Apollo 17 crewmen.

Chemical analysis of the orange soil material has shown the sample to be similar to one brought back from the Apollo 11 (Sea of Tranquillity) site several hundred kilometers to the southwest. Like it, this material is rich in titanium (8%) and iron oxide (22%). But unlike the Apollo 11 sample, the orange soil is inexplicably rich in zinc. The orange soil is probably of volcanic origin and not the product of meteorite impact.

CRATER A deep bowl-shaped depression in the surface of a body formed by the high-speed impact of another, smaller body.

CRYSTAL An ordered arrangement of molecules in a compound. Crystals that grow freely develop flat surfaces.

METEORITE A meteor that reaches the Earth's surface.

MICRON A millionth of a meter.

MINERAL A solid crystalline substance.

SILT Particles with a range of 2 microns to 60 microns across.

SOLAR WIND The flow of tiny charged particles (called plasma) outward from the Sun.

Analyzing the rocks

The rocks that were collected by both the American and Russian missions to the Moon have been invaluable in adding to our knowledge of the Moon and have helped in developing a model of how it formed.

For example, it has been possible to date the rocks using their **RADIOACTIVE** content. As soon as a rock cools, any radioactive **ISOTOPES** in it start to decay. If we know the rate of decay, the radioisotopes can be used as a geological clock.

Isotopes of rubidium and strontium can be used to date rocks that are billions of years old. Analysis of the lunar rocks showed conclusively that the Moon has a long history during which its components have formed into a **CRUST**, **MANTLE**, and **CORE**, and that many of the surface rocks are volcanic.

Highland rock samples were shown to be four billion years old. This proved the Moon's crust was already solid by then. Because the solar system is 4.6 billion years old, the formation of the Moon must therefore have occurred at an early date.

Samples of **MARE** lavas show that the volcanic rocks are much younger than the highland rocks, and so it is believed that after the Moon emerged, it heated up enough internally for liquid rock to form.

▲ This Apollo 16 lunar sample (usually just called "Moon rock") weighed 128 grams when returned to Earth (but just a sixth of that when collected on the Moon, due to the Moon's lower gravity).

The sample is a collection of broken fragments that have been fused together. This kind of rock is called a breccia.

This rock, like all lunar highland breccias, is very old (about 3.9 billion years), older than 99.99% of all Earth surface rocks.

The Moon's interior

What is not so obvious is anything about the Moon below the surface.

The Moon has an average **DENSITY** of 3.34 g/cm³. That is higher than the density of the Earth's crust and about the same as that of the Earth's mantle. It may possibly have a small metal core, but we simply don't know.

By studying its **ORBIT**, we know that the **CENTER OF GRAVITY** of the Moon is not quite in the center, but about 2 km toward the Earth. There are also more-dense and less-dense regions on the Moon's surface. The higher-density areas are called **MASCONS**. These facts have been determined by examining the pattern of **GRAVITY** of the Moon.

The Moon does not have a **MAGNETIC FIELD** like the Earth, which suggests that the core is not **MOLTEN** or moving. Nevertheless, Moon rocks do show some traces of **MAGNETISM**, and so a magnetic field did exist on the Moon in the past.

Many of these changes can be related to the fact that the Moon is so much smaller than the Earth. As a result, any heat it once had in its core has long ago flowed to the surface by **CONDUCTION** and been **RADIATED** to space.

Without this source of heat the churning movements of a molten core are not possible. Nonetheless, some very small "moon" quakes (seismic activities) still occur.

The point is, however, that the Moon was not always an inactive world. Certainly, billions of years ago the Moon quite suddenly became extremely hot, so much so that a crust formed over a core, and huge volcanoes sent lava flows over the surface. The mascons occur where the lava is thickest.

CENTER OF GRAVITY The point at which all of the mass of an object can be balanced.

CONDUCTION The transfer of heat between two objects when they touch.

CORE The central region of a body.

CRUST The solid outer surface of a rocky body.

DENSITY A measure of the amount of matter in a space.

GRAVITY The force of attraction between bodies.

ISOTOPE Atoms that have the same number of protons in their nucleus, but that have different masses; for example, carbon-12 and carbon-14.

MAGNETIC FIELD The region of influence of a magnetic body.

MAGNETISM An invisible force that has the property of attracting iron and similar metals.

MANTLE The region of a planet between the core and the crust.

MARE (pl. **MARIA**) A flat, dark plain created by lava flows. They were once thought to be seas.

MASCON A region of higher surface density on the Moon.

MOLTEN Liquid, suggesting that it has changed from a solid.

ORBIT The path followed by one object as it tracks around another.

RADIATE The transfer of energy in the form of waves (such as light and heat) or particles (such as from radioactive decay of a material).

RADIOACTIVE The property of some materials that emit radiation or energetic particles from the nucleus of their atoms.

▼ A possible internal structure for the Moon.

Asthenosphere. There may also be a metallic core.
60-100 km
Craters
about 740 km
1,740 km
Crust. Thickest on the side facing away from Earth.
Mare
Mantle (lithosphere)

Where the Moon came from

The Moon is a large space body very close to the Earth. At present the Moon and the Earth are moving apart, suggesting that they used to be much closer together.

Some people think that the Earth and the Moon formed at the same time, each building up from space debris.

Others believe that early on in the development of the Earth, when it was still liquid up to the surface, the spin was so fast that it threw off a lump, making the Moon.

But the Moon is much less dense than the Earth and so must have much less iron. That suggests the Moon and the Earth could not have come from the same body.

Then there is the idea that the Moon may have been captured from elsewhere in the solar system.

Most scientists now think the Moon was part of the early Earth. If this is true, then less than a billion years after the Earth had formed, it was struck a glancing blow by another planet perhaps as big as Mars. The collision, which destroyed the other planet, produced a huge amount of debris, which then formed into a ring around the Earth. This material then began to regroup as the Moon. As this happened, the material heated up, while at the same time, new bits of rock hit the surface of the newly forming Moon from the remaining debris cloud.

By about 3.9 billion years ago the Moon had cooled to produce a crust, and the craters we now see began to be preserved in the solid surface. About three billion years ago a long sequence of volcanic activity began that filled with lavas the basins on the side of the Moon facing the Earth.

These huge lava eruptions helped sap the heat from the Moon, and since then it has been more or less geologically inactive.

▼ These diagrams show how the Moon may have been formed.

1   **Planet crashes into Earth**

Another planet

Earth

2   **Ring of debris formed as other planet breaks up (mainly dust)**

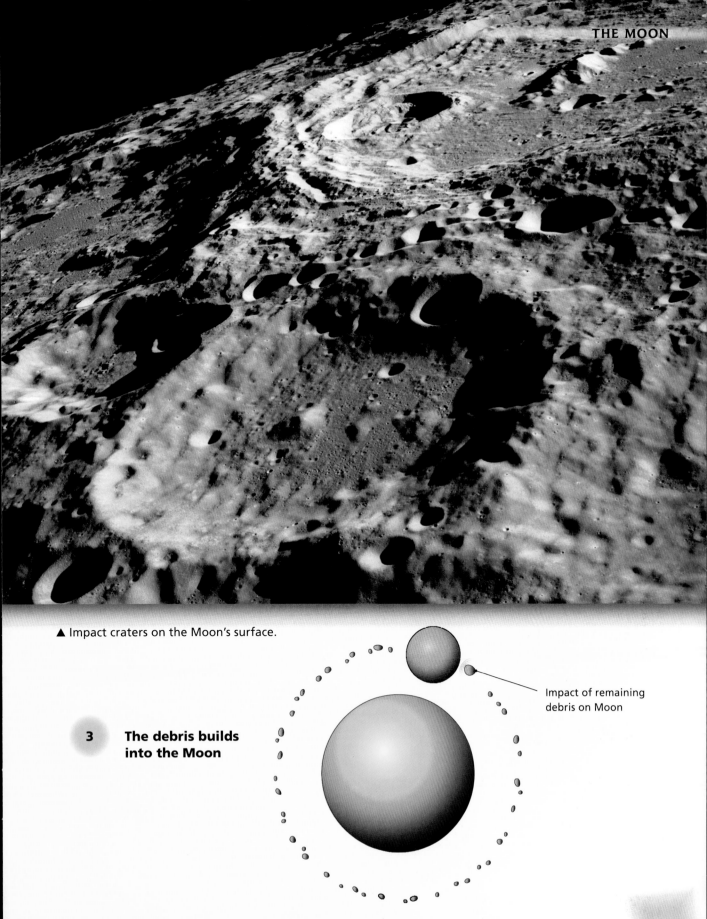

▲ Impact craters on the Moon's surface.

Impact of remaining
debris on Moon

3 **The debris builds
into the Moon**

SET GLOSSARY

Metric (SI) and U.S. standard unit conversion table

1 kilometer = 0.6 mile
1 meter = 3.3 feet or 1.1 yards
1 centimeter = 0.4 inch
1 tonne = (metric ton) 1,000
    kilograms, or 2,204.6 pounds
1 kilogram = 2.2 pounds
1 gram = 0.035 ounces

1 mile = 1.6 kilometers
1 foot = 0.3 meter
1 inch = 25.4 millimeters
    or 2.54 centimeters
1 ton = 907.18 kilograms
    in standard units,
    1,016.05 kilograms in metric
1 pound = 0.45 kilograms
1 ounce = 28 grams

$0°C = {}^5/9 (32°F)$

ABSOLUTE ZERO The coldest possible temperature, defined as 0 K or −273°C.
See also: **K.**

ACCELERATE To gain speed.

AERODYNAMIC A shape offering as little resistance to the air as possible.

AIR RESISTANCE The frictional drag that an object creates as it moves rapidly through the air.

AMINO ACIDS Simple organic molecules that can be building blocks for living things.

ANNULAR Ringlike.
    An annular eclipse occurs when the dark disk of the Moon does not completely obscure the Sun.

ANTENNA (pl. **ANTENNAE**) A device, often in the shape of a rod or wire, used for sending out and receiving radio waves.

ANTICLINE An arching fold of rock layers where the rocks slope down from the crest.

ANTICYCLONE A roughly circular region of the atmosphere that is spiraling outward and downward.

APOGEE The point on an orbit where the orbiting object is at its farthest from the object it is orbiting.

APOLLO The program developed in the United States by NASA to get people to the Moon's surface and back safely.

ARRAY A regular group or arrangement.

ASH Fragments of lava that have cooled and solidified between when they leave a volcano and when they fall to the surface.

ASTEROID Any of the many small objects within the solar system.
    Asteroids are rocky or metallic and are conventionally described as significant bodies with a diameter smaller than 1,000 km. Asteroids mainly occupy a belt between Mars and Jupiter (asteroid belt).

ASTEROID BELT The collection of asteroids that orbit the Sun between the orbits of Mars and Jupiter.

ASTHENOSPHERE The region below the lithosphere, and therefore part of the upper mantle, in which some material may be molten.

ASTRONOMICAL UNIT (**AU**) The average distance from the Earth to the Sun (149,597,870 km).

ASTRONOMY The study of space beyond the Earth and its contents. It includes those phenomena that affect the Earth but that originate in space, such as meteorites and aurora.

ASTROPHYSICS The study of physics in space, what other stars, galaxies, and planets are like, and the physical laws that govern them.

ASYNCHRONOUS Not connected in time or pace.

ATMOSPHERE The envelope of gases that surrounds the Earth and other bodies in the universe.
    The Earth's atmosphere is very different from that of other planets, being, for example, far lower in hydrogen and helium than the gas giants and lower in carbon dioxide than Venus, but richer in oxygen than all the others.

ATMOSPHERIC PRESSURE The pressure on the gases in the atmosphere caused by gravity pulling them toward the center of a celestial body.

ATOM The smallest particle of an element.

ATOMIC MASS UNIT A measure of the mass of an atom or molecule.
    An atomic mass unit equals one-twelfth of the mass of an atom of carbon-12.

ATOMIC WEAPONS Weapons that rely on the violent explosive force achieved when radioactive materials are made to go into an uncontrollable chain reaction.

ATOMIC WEIGHT The ratio of the average mass of a chemical element's atoms to carbon-12.

AURORA A region of illumination, often in the form of a wavy curtain, high in the atmosphere of a planet.
    It is the result of the interaction of the planet's magnetic field with the particles in the solar wind. High-energy electrons from the solar wind race along the planet's magnetic field into the upper atmosphere. The electrons excite atmospheric gases, making them glow.

AXIS (pl. **AXES**) The line around which a body spins.
    The Earth spins around an axis through its north and south geographic poles.

BALLISTIC MISSILE A rocket that is guided up in a high arching path; then the fuel supply is cut, and it is allowed to fall to the ground.

BASIN A large depression in the ground (bigger than a crater).

BIG BANG The theory that the universe as we know it started from a single point (called a singularity) and then exploded outward. It is still expanding today.

BINARY STAR A pair of stars that are gravitationally attracted, and that revolve around one another.

BLACK DWARF A degenerate star that has cooled so that it is now not visible.

BLACK HOLE An object that has a gravitational pull so strong that nothing can escape from it.
    A black hole may have a mass equal to thousands of stars or more.

BLUE GIANT A young, extremely bright and hot star of very large mass that has used up all its hydrogen and is no longer in the main sequence. When a blue giant ages, it becomes a red giant.

BOILING POINT The change of state of a substance in which a liquid rapidly turns into a gas without a change in temperature.

BOOSTER POD A form of housing that stands outside the main body of the launcher.

CALDERA A large pit in the top of a volcano produced when the top of the volcano explodes and collapses in on itself.

CAPSULE A small pressurized space vehicle.

CATALYST A substance that speeds up a chemical reaction but that is itself unchanged.

CELESTIAL Relating to the sky above, the "heavens."

CENTER OF GRAVITY The point at which all of the mass of an object can be balanced.

CENTRIFUGAL FORCE A force that acts on an orbiting or spinning body, tending to oppose gravity and move away from the center of rotation.
    For orbiting objects the centrifugal force acts in the opposite direction from gravity. When satellites orbit the Earth, the centrifugal force balances out the force of gravity.

CENTRIFUGE An instrument for spinning small samples very rapidly.

CHAIN REACTION A sequence of related events with one event triggering the next.

CHASM A deep, narrow trench.

CHROMOSPHERE The shell of gases that makes up part of the atmosphere of a star and lies between the photosphere and the corona.

CIRCUMFERENCE The distance around the edge of a circle or sphere.

COMA The blurred image caused by light bouncing from a collection of dust and ice particles escaping from the nucleus of a comet.

The coma changes the appearance of a comet from a point source of reflective light to a blurry object with a tail.

COMBUSTION CHAMBER A vessel inside an engine or motor where the fuel components mix and are set on fire, that is, they are burned (combusted).

COMET A small object, often described as being like a dirty snowball, that appears to be very bright in the night sky and has a long tail when it approaches the Sun.

Comets are thought to be some of the oldest objects in the solar system.

COMPLEMENTARY COLOR A color that is diametrically opposed in the range, or circle, of colors in the spectrum; for example, cyan (blue) is the complement of red.

COMPOSITE A material made from solid threads in a liquid matrix that is allowed to set.

COMPOUND A substance made from two or more elements that have chemically combined.

Ammonia is an example of a compound made from the elements hydrogen and nitrogen.

CONDENSE/CONDENSATION (1) To make something more concentrated or compact.

(2) The change of state from a gas or vapor to a liquid.

CONDUCTION The transfer of heat between two objects when they touch.

CONSTELLATION One of many commonly recognized patterns of stars in the sky.

CONVECTION/CONVECTION CURRENTS The circulating flow in a fluid (liquid or gas) that occurs when it is heated from below.

Convective flow is caused in a fluid by the tendency for hotter, and therefore less dense, material to rise and for colder, and therefore more dense, material, to sink with gravity. That results in a heat transfer.

CORE The central region of a body.

The core of the Earth is about 3,300 km in radius, compared with the radius of the whole Earth, which is 6,300 km.

CORONA (pl. **CORONAE**) (1) A colored circle seen around a bright object such as a star.

(2) The gases surrounding a star such as the Sun. In the case of the Sun and certain other stars these gases are extremely hot.

(3) A circular to oval pattern of faults, fractures, and ridges with a sagging center as found on Venus. In the case of Venus they are a few hundred kilometers in diameter.

CORONAL MASS EJECTIONS Very large bubbles of plasma escaping into the corona.

CORROSIVE SUBSTANCE Something that chemically eats away something else.

COSMOLOGICAL PRINCIPLE States that the way you see the universe is independent of the place where you are (your location). In effect, it means that the universe is roughly uniform throughout.

COSMONAUT A Russian space person.

COSMOS The universe and everything in it. The word "cosmos" suggests that the universe operates according to orderly principles.

CRATER A deep bowl-shaped depression in the surface of a body formed by the high-speed impact of another, smaller body.

Most craters are formed by the impact of asteroids and meteoroids. Craters have both a depression, or pit, and also an elevated rim formed of the material displaced from the central pit.

CRESCENT The appearance of the Moon when it is between a new Moon and a half Moon.

CRUST The solid outer surface of a rocky body.

The crust of the Earth is mainly just a few tens of kilometers thick, compared to the total radius of 6,300 km for the whole Earth. It forms much of the lithosphere.

CRYSTAL An ordered arrangement of molecules in a compound. Crystals that grow freely develop flat surfaces.

CYCLONE A large storm in which the atmosphere spirals inward and upward.

On Earth cyclones have a very low atmospheric pressure at their center and often contain deep clouds.

DARK MATTER Matter that does not shine or reflect light.

No one has ever found dark matter, but it is thought to exist because the amount of ordinary matter in the universe is not enough to account for many gravitational effects that have been observed.

DENSITY A measure of the amount of matter in a space.

Density is often measured in grams per cubic centimeter. The density of the Earth is 5.5 grams per cubic centimeter.

DEORBIT To move out of an orbital position and begin a reentry path toward the Earth.

DEPRESSION (1) A sunken area or hollow in a surface or landscape.

(2) A region of inward swirling air in the atmosphere associated with cloudy weather and rain.

DIFFRACTION The bending of light as it goes through materials of different density.

DISK A shape or surface that looks round and flat.

DOCK To meet with and attach to another space vehicle.

DOCKING PORT/STATION A place on the side of a spacecraft that contains some form of anchoring mechanism and an airlock.

DOPPLER EFFECT The apparent change in pitch of a fast-moving object as it approaches or leaves an observer.

DOWNLINK A communication to Earth from a spacecraft.

DRAG A force that hinders the movement of something.

DWARF STAR A star that shines with a brightness that is average or below.

EARTH The third planet from the Sun and the one on which we live.

The Earth belongs to the group of rocky planets. It is unique in having an oxygen-rich atmosphere and water, commonly found in its three phases—solid, liquid, and gas.

EARTHQUAKE The shock waves produced by the sudden movement of two pieces of brittle crust.

ECCENTRIC A noncircular, or oval, orbit.

ECLIPSE The time when light is cut off by a body coming between the observer and the source of the illumination (for example, eclipse of the Sun), or when the body the observer is on comes between the source of illumination and another body (for example, eclipse of the Moon).

It happens when three bodies are in a line. This phenomenon is not necessarily called an eclipse. Occultations of stars by the Moon and transits of Venus or Mercury are examples of different expressions used instead of "eclipse."

See also: **TOTAL ECLIPSE.**

ECOLOGY The study of living things in their environment.

ELECTRONS Negatively charged particles that are parts of atoms.

ELEMENT A substance that cannot be decomposed into simpler substances by chemical means.

Elements are the building blocks of compounds. For example, silicon and oxygen are elements. They combine to form the compound silicon dioxide, or quartz.

ELLIPTICAL GALAXY A galaxy that has an oval shape rather like a football, and that has no spiral arms.

EL NIÑO A time when ocean currents in the Pacific Ocean reverse from their normal pattern and disrupt global weather patterns. It occurs once every 4 or 5 years.

EMISSION Something that is sent or let out.

ENCKE GAP A gap between rings around Saturn named for the astronomer Johann Franz Encke (1791–1865).

EPOXY RESIN Adhesives that develop their strength as they react, or "cure," after mixing.

EQUATOR The ring drawn around a body midway between the poles.

EQUILIBRIUM A state of balance.

ESA The European Space Agency. ESA is an organizaton of European countries for cooperation in space research and technology. It operates several installations around Europe and has its headquarters in Paris, France.

ESCARPMENT A sharp-edged ridge.

EVAPORATE/EVAPORATION The change in state from liquid to a gas.

EXOSPHERE The outer part of the atmosphere starting about 500 km from the surface. This layer contains so little air that molecules rarely collide.

EXTRAVEHICULAR ACTIVITY Any task performed by people outside the protected environment of a space vehicle's pressurized compartments. Extravehicular activities (EVA) include repairing equipment in the Space Shuttle bay.

FALSE COLOR The colors used to make the appearance of some property more obvious.
They are part of the computer generation of an image.

FAULT A place in the crust where rocks have fractured, and then one side has moved relative to the other.
A fault is caused by excessive pressure on brittle rocks.

FLUORESCENT Emitting the visible light produced by a substance when it is struck by invisible waves, such as ultraviolet waves.

FRACTURE A break in brittle rock.

FREQUENCY The number of complete cycles of (for example, radio) waves received per second.

FRICTION The force that resists two bodies that are in contact.
For example, the effect of the ocean waters moving as tides slows the Earth's rotation.

FUSION The joining of atomic nuclei to form heavier nuclei.
This process results in the release of huge amounts of energy.

GALAXY A system of stars and interstellar matter within the universe.
Galaxies may contain billions of stars.

GALILEAN SATELLITES The four large satellites of Jupiter discovered by astronomer Galileo Galilei in 1610. They are Callisto, Europa, Ganymede, and Io.

GALILEO A U.S. space probe launched in October 1989 and designed for intensive investigation of Jupiter.

GEIGER TUBE A device to detect radioactive materials.

GEOSTATIONARY ORBIT A circular orbit 35,786 km directly above the Earth's equator.
Communications satellites frequently use this orbit. A satellite in a geostationary orbit will move at the same rate as the Earth's rotation, completing one revolution in 24 hours. That way it remains at the same point over the Earth's equator.

GEOSTATIONARY SATELLITE A man-made satellite in a fixed or geosynchronous orbit around the Earth.

GEOSYNCHRONOUS ORBIT An orbit in which a satellite makes one circuit of the Earth in 24 hours.
A geosynchronous orbit coincides with the Earth's orbit—it takes the same time to complete an orbit as it does for the Earth to make one complete rotation. If the orbit is circular and above the equator, then the satellite remains over one particular point of the equator; that is called a geostationary orbit.

GEOSYNCLINE A large downward sag or trench that forms in the Earth's crust as a result of colliding tectonic plates.

GEYSER A periodic fountain of material. On Earth geysers are of water and steam, but on other planets and moons they are formed from other substances, for example, nitrogen gas on Triton.

GIBBOUS When between half and a full disk of a body can be seen lighted by the Sun.

GIMBALS A framework that allows anything inside it to move in a variety of directions.

GLOBAL POSITIONING SYSTEM A network of geostationary satellites that can be used to locate the position of any object on the Earth's surface.

GRANULATION The speckled pattern we see in the Sun's photosphere as a result of convectional overturning of gases.

GRAVITATIONAL FIELD The region surrounding a body in which that body's gravitational force can be felt.
The gravitational field of the Sun spreads over the entire solar system. The gravitational fields of the planets each exert some influence on the orbits of their neighbors.

GRAVITY/GRAVITATIONAL FORCE/ GRAVITATIONAL PULL The force of attraction between bodies. The larger an object, the more its gravitational pull on other objects.
The Sun's gravity is the most powerful in the solar system, keeping all of the planets and other materials within the solar system.

GREAT RED SPOT A large, almost permanent feature of the Jovian atmosphere that moves around the planet at about latitude 23°S.

GREENHOUSE EFFECT The increase in atmospheric temperature produced by the presence of carbon dioxide in the air.
Carbon dioxide has the ability to soak up heat radiated from the surface of a planet and partly prevent its escape. The effect is similar to that produced by a greenhouse.

GROUND STATION A receiving and transmitting station in direct communication with satellites. Such stations are characterized by having large dish-shaped antennae.

GULLY (pl. **GULLIES**) A trench in the land surface formed, on Earth, by running water.

GYROSCOPE A device in which a rapidly spinning wheel is held in a frame in such a way that it can rotate in any direction. The momentum of the wheel means that the gyroscope retains its position even when the frame is tilted.

HEAT SHIELD A protective device on the outside of a space vehicle that absorbs the heat during reentry and protects it from burning up.

HELIOPAUSE The edge of the heliosphere.

HELIOSEISMOLOGY The study of the internal structure of the Sun by modeling the Sun's patterns of internal shock waves.

HELIOSPHERE The entire range of influence of the Sun. It extends to the edge of the solar system.

HUBBLE SPACE TELESCOPE An orbiting telescope (and so a satellite) that was placed above the Earth's atmosphere so that it could take images that were far clearer than anything that could be obtained from the surface of the Earth.

HURRICANE A very violent cyclone that begins close to the equator, and that contains winds of over 117 km/hr.

ICE CAP A small mountainous region that is covered in ice.

INFRARED Radiation with a wavelength that is longer than red light.

INNER PLANETS The rocky planets closest to the Sun. They are Mercury, Venus, Earth, and Mars.

INTERNATIONAL SPACE STATION The international orbiting space laboratory.

INTERPLANETARY DUST The fine dustlike material that lies scattered through space, and that exists between the planets as well as in outer space.

INTERSTELLAR Between the stars.

IONIZED Matter that has been converted into small charged particles called ions.
An atom that has gained or lost an electron.

IONOSPHERE A part of the Earth's atmosphere in which the number of ions (electrically charged particles) is enough to affect how radio waves move.
The ionosphere begins about 50 km above the Earth's surface.

IRREGULAR SATELLITES Satellites that orbit in the opposite direction from their parent planet.
This motion is also called retrograde rotation.

ISOTOPE Atoms that have the same number of protons in their nucleus, but that have different masses; for example, carbon-12 and carbon-14.

JOVIAN PLANETS An alternative group name for the gas giant planets: Jupiter, Saturn, Uranus, and Neptune.

JUPITER The fifth planet from the Sun and two planets farther away from the Sun than the Earth.
Jupiter is 318 times as massive as the Earth and 1,500 times as big by volume. It is the largest of the gas giants.

K Named for British scientist Lord Kelvin (1824–1907), it is a measurement of absolute temperature. Zero K is called absolute zero and is only approached in deep space: ice melts at 273 K, and water boils at 373 K.

KEELER GAP A gap in the rings of Saturn named for the astronomer James Edward Keeler (1857–1900).

KILOPARSEC A unit of a thousand parsecs. A parsec is the unit used for measuring the largest distances in the universe.

KUIPER BELT A belt of planetesimals (small rocky bodies, one kilometer to hundreds of kilometers across) much closer to the Sun than the Oort cloud.

LANDSLIDE A sudden collapse of material on a steep slope.

LA NIÑA Below normal ocean temperatures in the eastern Pacific Ocean that disrupt global weather patterns.

LATITUDE Angular distance north or south of the equator, measured through 90°.

LAUNCH VEHICLE/LAUNCHER A system of propellant tanks and rocket motors or engines designed to lift a payload into space. It may, or may not, be part of a space vehicle.

LAVA Hot, melted rock from a volcano.
Lava flows onto the surface of a planet and cools and hardens to form new rock. Most of the lava on Earth is made of basalt.

LAVA FLOW A river or sheet of liquid volcanic rock.

LAWS OF MOTION Formulated by Sir Isaac Newton, they describe the forces that act on a moving object.
The first law states that an object will keep moving in a straight line at constant speed unless it is acted on by a force.
The second law states that the force on an object is related to the mass of the object multiplied by its acceleration.
The third law states that an action always has an equal and directly opposite reaction.

LIFT An upthrust on the wing of a plane that occurs when it moves rapidly through the air. It is the main way of suspending an airplane during flight. The engines simply provide the forward thrust.

LIGHT-YEAR The distance traveled by light through space in one Earth year, or 63,240 astronomical units.
The speed of light is the speed that light travels through a vacuum, which is 299,792 km/s.

LIMB The outer edge of a celestial body, including an atmosphere if it has one.

LITHOSPHERE The upper part of the Earth, corresponding generally to the crust and believed to be about 80 km thick.

LOCAL GROUP The Milky Way, the Magellanic Clouds, the Andromeda Galaxy, and over 20 other relatively near galaxies.

LUNAR Anything to do with the Moon.

MAGELLANIC CLOUD Either of two small galaxies that are companions to the Milky Way Galaxy.

MAGMA Hot, melted rock inside the Earth that, when cooled, forms igneous rock.
Magma is associated with volcanic activity.

MAGNETIC FIELD The region of influence of a magnetic body.

The Earth's magnetic field stretches out beyond the atmosphere into space. There it interacts with the solar wind to produce auroras.

MAGNETISM An invisible force that has the property of attracting iron and similar metals.

MAGNETOPAUSE The outer edge of the magnetosphere.

MAGNETOSPHERE A region in the upper atmosphere, or around a planet, where magnetic phenomena such as auroras are found.

MAGNITUDE A measure of the brightness of a star.
The apparent magnitude is the brightness of a celestial object as seen from the Earth. The absolute magnitude is the standardized brightness measured as though all objects were the same distance from the Earth. The brighter the object, the lower its magnitude number. For example, a star of magnitude 4 is 2.5 times as bright as one of magnitude 5. A difference of five magnitudes is the same as a difference in brightness of 100 to 1. The brightest stars have negative numbers. The Sun's apparent magnitude is −26.8. Its absolute magnitude is 4.8.

MAIN SEQUENCE The 90% of stars in the universe that represent the mature phase of stars with small or medium mass.

MANTLE The region of a planet between the core and the crust.
The Earth's mantle is about 2,900 km thick, and its upper surface may be molten in some places.

MARE (pl. **MARIA**) A flat, dark plain created by lava flows. They were once thought to be seas.

MARS The fourth planet from the Sun in our solar system and one planet farther away from the Sun than the Earth.
Mars is a rocky planet almost half the diameter of Earth that is a distinctive rust-red color.

MASCON A region of higher surface density on the Moon.

MASS The amount of matter in an object.
The amount of matter, and so the mass, remains the same, but the effect of gravity gives the mass a weight. The weight depends on the gravitational pull. Thus a ball will have the same mass on the Earth and on the Moon, but it will weigh a sixth as much on the Moon because the force of gravity there is only a sixth as strong.

MATTER Anything that exists in physical form.
Everything we can see is made of matter. The building blocks of matter are atoms.

MERCURY The closest planet to the Sun in our solar system and two planets closer to the Sun than Earth.
Mercury is a gray-colored rocky planet less than half the diameter of Earth. It has the most extreme temperature range of any planet in our solar system.

MESOSPHERE One of the upper regions of the atmosphere, beginning at the top of the stratosphere and continuing from 50 km upward until the temperature stops declining.

METEOR A streak of light (shooting star) produced by a meteoroid as it enters the Earth's atmosphere.
The friction with the Earth's atmosphere causes the small body to glow (become incandescent). That is what we see as a streak of light.

METEORITE A meteor that reaches the Earth's surface.

METEOROID A small body moving in the solar system that becomes a meteor if it enters the Earth's atmosphere.
Meteoroids are typically only a few millimeters across and burn up as they go through the atmosphere, but some have crashed to the Earth, making large craters.

MICROMETEORITES Tiny pieces of space dust moving at high speeds.

MICRON A millionth of a meter.

MICROWAVELENGTH Waves at the shortest end of the radio wavelengths.

MICROWAVE RADIATION The background radiation that is found everywhere in space, and whose existence is used to support the Big Bang theory.

MILKY WAY The spiral galaxy in which our star and solar system are situated.

MINERAL A solid crystalline substance.

MINOR PLANET Another term for an asteroid.

M NUMBER In 1781 Charles Messier began a catalogue of the objects he could see in the night sky. He gave each of them a unique number. The first entry was called M1. There is no significance to the number in terms of brightness, size, closeness, or otherwise.

MODULE A section, or part, of a space vehicle.

MOLECULE A group of two or more atoms held together by chemical bonds.

MOLTEN Liquid, suggesting that it has changed from a solid.

MOMENTUM The mass of an object multiplied by its velocity.

MOON The natural satellite that orbits the Earth.
Other planets have large satellites, or moons, but none is relatively as large as our Moon, suggesting that it has a unique origin.

MOON The name generally given to any large natural satellite of a planet.

MOUNTAIN RANGE A long, narrow region of very high land that contains several or many mountains.

NASA The National Aeronautics and Space Administration.
NASA was founded in 1958 for aeronautical and space exploration. It operates several installations around the country and has its headquarters in Washington, D.C.

NEAP TIDE A tide showing the smallest difference between high and low tides.

NEBULA (pl. **NEBULAE**) Clouds of gas and dust that exist in the space between stars.

The word means mist or cloud and is also used as an alternative to galaxy. The gas makes up to 5% of the mass of a galaxy. What a nebula looks like depends on the arrangement of gas and dust within it.

NEPTUNE The eighth planet from the Sun in our solar system and five planets farther away from the Sun than the Earth.

Neptune is a gas planet that is almost four times the diameter of Earth. It is blue.

NEUTRINOS An uncharged fundamental particle that is thought to have no mass.

NEUTRONS Particles inside the core of an atom that are neutral (have no charge).

NEUTRON STAR A very dense star that consists only of tightly packed neutrons. It is the result of the collapse of a massive star.

NOBLE GASES The unreactive gases, such as neon, xenon, and krypton.

NOVA (pl. **NOVAE**) (1) A star that suddenly becomes much brighter, then fades away to its original brightness within a few months.
See also: SUPERNOVA.

(2) A radiating pattern of faults and fractures unique to Venus.

NUCLEAR DEVICES Anything that is powered by a source of radioactivity.

NUCLEUS (pl. **NUCLEI**) The centermost part of something, the core.

OORT CLOUD A region on the edge of the solar system that consists of planetesimals and comets that did not get caught up in planet making.

OPTICAL Relating to the use of light.

ORBIT The path followed by one object as it tracks around another.

The orbits of the planets around the Sun and moons around their planets are oval, or elliptical.

ORGANIC MATERIAL Any matter that contains carbon and is alive.

OUTER PLANETS The gas giant planets Jupiter, Saturn, Uranus, and Neptune plus the rocky planet Pluto.

OXIDIZER The substance in a reaction that removes electrons from and thereby oxidizes (burns) another substance.

In the case of oxygen this results in the other substance combining with the oxygen to form an oxide (also called an oxidizing agent).

OZONE A form of oxygen (O_3) with three atoms in each molecule instead of the more usual two (O_2).

OZONE HOLE The observed lack of the gas ozone in the upper atmosphere.

PARSEC The unit used for measuring the largest distances in the universe.

A parsec is the distance at which an observer in space would see the radius of the orbit as making one second of arc. This gives a distance of about 3.26 light-years.
See also: KILOPARSEC.

PAYLOAD The spacecraft that is carried into space by a launcher.

PENUMBRA (1) A region that is in semidarkness during an eclipse.

(2) The part of a sunspot surrounding the umbra.

PERCOLATE To flow by gravity between particles, for example, of soil.

PERIGEE The point on an orbit where the orbiting object is as close as it ever comes to the object it is orbiting.

PHARMACEUTICAL Relating to medicinal drugs.

PHASE The differing appearance of a body that is closer to the Sun, and that is illuminated by it.

PHOTOCHEMICAL SMOG A hazy atmosphere, often brown, resulting from the reaction of nitrogen gases with sunlight.

PHOTOMOSAIC A composite picture made up of several other pictures that individually only cover a small area.

PHOTON A particle (quantum) of electromagnetic radiation.

PHOTOSPHERE A shell of the Sun that we regard as its visible surface.

PHOTOSYNTHESIS The process that plants use to combine the substances in the environment, such as carbon dioxide, minerals, and water, with oxygen and energy-rich organic compounds by using the energy of sunlight.

PIONEER A name for a series of unmanned U.S. spacecraft.

Pioneer 1 was launched into lunar orbit on October 11, 1958. The others all went into deep space.

PLAIN A flat or gently rolling part of a landscape.

Plains are confined to lowlands. If a flat surface exists in an upland, it is called a plateau.

PLANE A flat surface.

PLANET Any of the large bodies that orbit the Sun.

The planets are (outward from the Sun): Mercury, Venus, Earth, Mars, Jupiter, Saturn, Uranus, Neptune, and Pluto. The rocky planets all have densities greater than 3 grams per cubic centimeter; the gaseous ones less than 2 grams per cubic centimeter.

PLANETARY NEBULA A compact ring or oval nebula that is made of material thrown out of a hot star.

The term "planetary nebula" is a misnomer; dying stars create these cocoons when they lose outer layers of gas. The process has nothing to do with planet formation, which is predicted to happen early in a star's life.

The term originates from a time when people, looking through weak telescopes, thought that the nebulae resembled planets within the solar system, when in fact they were expanding shells of glowing gas in far-off galaxies.

PLANETESIMAL Small rocky bodies one kilometer to hundreds of kilometers across.

The word especially relates to materials that exist in the early stages of the formation of a star and its planets from the dust of a nebula, which will eventually group together to form planets. Some are rock, others a mixture of rock and ice.

PLANKTON Microscopic creatures that float in water.

PLASMA A collection of charged particles that behaves something like a gas. It can conduct an electric charge and be affected by magnetic fields.

PLASTIC The ability of certain solid substances to be molded or deformed to a new shape under pressure without cracking.

PLATE A very large unbroken part of the crust of a planet. Also called tectonic plate.

On Earth the tectonic plates are dragged across the surface by convection currents in the underlying mantle.

PLATEAU An upland plain or tableland.

PLUTO The ninth planet from the Sun and six planets farther from the Sun than the Earth.

Pluto is one of the rocky planets, but it is very different from the others, perhaps being a mixture of rock and ice. It is about two-thirds the size of our Moon.

POLE The geographic pole is the place where a line drawn along the axis of rotation exits from a body's surface.

Magnetic poles do not always correspond with geographic poles.

POLYMER A compound that is made up of long chains formed by combining molecules called monomers as repeating units. ("Poly" means many, "mer" means part.)

PRESSURE The force per unit area.

PROBE An unmanned spacecraft designed to explore our solar system and beyond.

Voyager, Cassini, and Magellan are examples of probes.

PROJECTILE An object propelled through the air or space by an external force or an on-board engine.

PROMINENCE A cloud of burning ionized gas that rises through the Sun's chromosphere into the corona. It can take the form of a sheet or a loop.

PROPELLANT A gas, liquid, or solid that can be expelled rapidly from the end of an object in order to give it motion.

Liquefied gases and solids are used as rocket propellants.

PROPULSION SYSTEM The motors or rockets and their tanks designed to give a launcher or space vehicle the thrust it needs.

PROTEIN Molecules in living things that are vital for building tissues.

PROTONS Positively charged particles from the core of an atom.

PROTOSTAR A cloud of gas and dust that begins to swirl around; the resulting gravity gives birth to a star.

PULSAR A neutron star that is spinning around, releasing electromagnetic radiation, including radio waves.

QUANTUM THEORY A concept of how energy can be divided into tiny pieces called quanta, which is the key to how the smallest particles work and how they build together to make the universe around us.

QUASAR A rare starlike object of enormous brightness that gives out radio waves, which are thought to be released as material is sucked toward a black hole.

RADAR Short for radio detecting and ranging. A system of bouncing radio waves from objects in order to map their surfaces and find out how far away they are.

Radar is useful in conditions where visible light cannot be used.

RADIATION/RADIATE The transfer of energy in the form of waves (such as light and heat) or particles (such as from radioactive decay of a material).

RADIOACTIVE/RADIOACTIVITY The property of some materials that emit radiation or energetic particles from the nucleus of their atoms.

RADIOACTIVE DECAY The change that takes place inside radioactive materials and causes them to give out progressively less radiation over time.

RADIO GALAXY A galaxy that gives out radio waves of enormous power.

RADIO INTERFERENCE Reduction in the radio communication effectiveness of the ionosphere caused by sunspots and other increases in the solar wind.

RADIO TELESCOPE A telescope that is designed to detect radio waves rather than light waves.

RADIO WAVES A form of electromagnetic radiation, like light and heat. Radio waves have a longer wavelength than light waves.

RADIUS (pl. **RADII**) The distance from the center to the outside of a circle or sphere.

RAY A line across the surface of a planet or moon made by material from a crater being flung across the surface.

REACTION An opposition to a force.

REACTIVE The ability of a chemical substance to combine readily with other substances. Oxygen is an example of a reactive substance.

RED GIANT A cool, large, bright star at least 25 times the diameter of our Sun.

REFLECT/REFLECTION/REFLECTIVE To bounce back any light that falls on a surface.

REGULAR SATELLITES Satellites that orbit in the same direction as their parent planet. This motion is also called synchronous rotation.

RESOLVING POWER The ability of an optical telescope to form an image of a distant object.

RETROGRADE DIRECTION An orbit the opposite of normal—that is, a planet that spins so the Sun rises in the west and sinks in the east.

RETROROCKET A rocket that fires against the direction of travel in order to slow down a space vehicle.

RIDGE A narrow crest of an upland area.

RIFT A trench made by the sinking of a part of the crust between parallel faults.

RIFT VALLEY A long trench in the surface of a planet produced by the collapse of the crust in a narrow zone.

ROCKET Any kind of device that uses the principle of jet propulsion, that is, the rapid release of gases designed to propel an object rapidly.

The word is also applied loosely to fireworks and spacecraft launch vehicles.

ROCKET ENGINE A propulsion system that burns liquid fuel such as liquid hydrogen.

ROCKET MOTOR A propulsion system that burns solid fuel such as hydrazine.

ROCKETRY Experimentation with rockets.

ROTATION Spinning around an axis.

SAND DUNE An aerodynamically shaped hump of sand.

SAROS CYCLE The interval of 18 years $11^1/3$ days needed for the Earth, Sun, and Moon to come back into the same relative positions. It controls the pattern of eclipses.

SATELLITE (1) An object that is in an orbit around another object, usually a planet.

The Moon is a satellite of the Earth.
See also: **IRREGULAR SATELLITE, MOON, GALILEAN SATELLITE, REGULAR SATELLITE, SHEPHERD SATELLITE.**

(2) A man-made object that orbits the Earth. Usually used as a term for an unmanned spacecraft whose job is to acquire or transfer data to and from the ground.

SATURN The sixth planet from the Sun and three planets farther away from the Sun than the Earth.

It is the least-dense planet in the solar system, having 95 times the mass of the Earth, but 766 times the volume. It is one of the gas giant planets.

SCARP The steep slope of a sharp-crested ridge.

SEASONS The characteristic cycle of events in the heating of the Earth that causes related changes in weather patterns.

SEDIMENT Any particles of material that settle out, usually in layers, from a moving fluid such as air or water.

SEDIMENTARY Rocks deposited in layers.

SEISMIC Shaking, relating to earthquakes.

SENSOR A device used to detect something. Your eyes, ears, and nose are all sensors. Satellites use sensors that mainly detect changes in radio and other waves, including sunlight.

SHEPHERD SATELLITES Larger natural satellites that have an influence on small debris in nearby rings because of their gravity.

SHIELD VOLCANO A volcanic cone that is broad and gently sloping.

SIDEREAL MONTH The average time that the Moon takes to return to the same position against the background of stars.

SILT Particles with a range of 2 microns to 60 microns across.

SLINGSHOT TRAJECTORY A path chosen to use the attractive force of gravity to increase the speed of a spacecraft.

The craft is flown toward the planet or star, and it speeds up under the gravitational force. At the correct moment the path is taken to send the spacecraft into orbit and, when pointing in the right direction, to turn it from orbit, with its increased velocity, toward the final destination.

SOLAR Anything to do with the Sun.

SOLAR CELL A photoelectric device that converts the energy from the Sun (solar radiation) into electrical energy.

SOLAR FLARE Any sudden explosion from the surface of the Sun that sends ultraviolet radiation into the chromosphere. It also sends out some particles that reach Earth and disrupt radio communications.

SOLAR PANELS Large flat surfaces covered with thousands of small photoelectric devices that convert solar radiation into electricity.

SOLAR RADIATION The light and heat energy sent into space from the Sun.

Visible light and heat are just two of the many forms of energy sent by the Sun to the Earth.

SOLAR SYSTEM The Sun and the bodies orbiting around it.

The solar system contains nine major planets, at least 60 moons (large natural satellites), and a vast number of asteroids and comets, together with the gases within the system.

SOLAR WIND The flow of tiny charged particles (called plasma) outward from the Sun.

The solar wind stretches out across the solar system.

SONIC BOOM The noise created when an object moves faster than the speed of sound.

SPACE Everything beyond the Earth's atmosphere.

The word "space" is used rather generally. It can be divided up into inner space—the solar system, and outer space—everything beyond the solar system, for example, interstellar space.

SPACECRAFT Anything capable of moving beyond the Earth's atmosphere. Spacecraft can be manned or unmanned. Unmanned spacecraft are often referred to as space probes if they are exploring new areas.

SPACE RACE The period from the 1950s to the 1970s when the United States and the Soviet Union competed to be first in achievements in space.

SPACE SHUTTLE NASA's reusable space vehicle that is launched like a rocket but returns like a glider.

SPACE STATION A large man-made satellite used as a base for operations in space.

SPEED OF LIGHT *See:* **LIGHT-YEAR**.

SPHERE A ball-shaped object.

SPICULES Jets of relatively cool gas that move upward through the chromosphere into the corona.

SPIRAL GALAXY A galaxy that has a core of stars at the center of long curved arms made of even more stars arranged in a spiral shape.

SPRING TIDE A tide showing the greatest difference between high and low tides.

STAR A large ball of gases that radiates light. The star nearest the Earth is the Sun.

There are enormous numbers of stars in the universe, but few can be seen with the naked eye. Stars may occur singly, as our Sun, or in groups, of which pairs are most common.

STAR CLUSTER A group of gravitationally connected stars.

STELLAR WIND The flow of tiny charged particles (called plasma) outward from a star.

In our solar system the stellar wind is the same as the solar wind.

STRATOSPHERE The region immediately above the troposphere where the temperature increases with height, and the air is always stable.

It acts like an invisible lid, keeping the clouds in the troposphere.

SUBDUCTION ZONES Long, relatively thin, but very deep regions of the crust where one plate moves down and under, or subducts, another. They are the source of mountain ranges.

SUN The star that the planets of the solar system revolve around.

The Sun is 150 million km from the Earth and provides energy (in the form of light and heat) to our planet. Its density of 1.4 grams per cubic centimeter is similar to that of a gas giant planet.

SUNSPOT A spiral of gas found on the Sun that is moving slowly upward, and that is cooler than the surrounding gas and so looks darker.

SUPERNOVA A violently exploding star that becomes millions or even billions of times brighter than when it was younger and stable.

See also: **NOVA**.

SYNCHRONOUS Taking place at the same time.

SYNCHRONOUS ORBIT An orbit in which a satellite (such as a moon) moves around a planet in the same time that it takes for the planet to make one rotation on its axis.

SYNCHRONOUS ROTATION When two bodies make a complete rotation on their axes in the same time.

As a result, each body always has the same side facing the other. The Moon and Venus are in synchronous rotation with the Earth.

SYNODIC MONTH The complete cycle of phases of the Moon as seen from Earth. It is 29.531 solar days (29 days, 12 hours, 44 minutes, 3 seconds).

SYNODIC PERIOD The time needed for an object within the solar system, such as a planet, to return to the same place relative to the Sun as seen from the Earth.

TANGENT A direction at right angles to a line radiating from a circle or sphere.

If you make a wheel spin, for example, by repeatedly giving it a glancing blow with your hand, the glancing blow is moving along a tangent.

TELECOMMUNICATIONS Sending messages by means of telemetry, using signals made into waves such as radio waves.

THEORY OF RELATIVITY A theory based on how physical laws change when an observer is moving. Its most famous equation says that at the speed of light, energy is related to mass and the speed of light.

THERMOSPHERE A region of the upper atmosphere above the mesosphere.

It absorbs ultraviolet radiation and is where the ionosphere has most effect.

THRUST A very strong and continued pressure.

THRUSTER A term for a small rocket engine.

TIDE Any kind of regular, or cyclic, change that occurs due to the effect of the gravity of one body on another.

We are used to the ocean waters of the Earth being affected by the gravitational pull of the Moon, but tides also cause a small alteration of the shape of a body. This is important in determining the shape of many moons and may even be a source of heating in some.

See also: **NEAP TIDE** and **SPRING TIDE**.

TOPOGRAPHY The shape of the land surface in terms of height.

TOTAL ECLIPSE When one body (such as the Moon or Earth) completely obscures the light source from another body (such as the Earth or Moon).

A total eclipse of the Sun occurs when it is completely blocked out by the Moon.

A total eclipse of the Moon occurs when it passes into the Earth's shadow to such a degree that light from the Sun is completely blocked out.

TRAJECTORY The curved path followed by a projectile.

See also: **SLINGSHOT TRAJECTORY**.

TRANSPONDER Wireless receiver and transmitter.

TROPOSPHERE The lowest region of the atmosphere, where all of the Earth's clouds form.

TRUSS Tubing arrayed in the form of triangles and designed to make a strong frame.

ULTRAVIOLET A form of radiation that is just beyond the violet end of the visible spectrum and so is called "ultra" (more than) violet. At the other end of the visible spectrum is "infra" (less than) red.

UMBRA (1) A region that is in complete darkness during an eclipse.

(2) The darkest region in the center of a sunspot.

UNIVERSE The entirety of everything there is; the cosmos.

Many space scientists prefer to use the term "cosmos," referring to the entirety of energy and matter.

UNSTABLE In atmospheric terms the potential churning of the air in the atmosphere as a result of air being heated from below. There is a chance of the warmed, less-dense air rising through the overlying colder, more-dense air.

UPLINK A communication from Earth to a spacecraft.

URANUS The seventh planet from the Sun and four planets farther from the Sun than the Earth.

Its diameter is four times that of the Earth. It is one of the gas giant planets.

VACUUM A space that is entirely empty. A vacuum lacks any matter.

VALLEY A natural long depression in the landscape.

VELOCITY A more precise word to describe how something is moving, because movement has both a magnitude (speed) and a direction.

VENT The tube or fissure that allows volcanic materials to reach the surface of a planet.

VENUS The second planet from the Sun and our closest neighbor.

It appears as an evening and morning "star" in the sky. Venus is very similar to the Earth in size and mass.

VOLCANO A mound or mountain that is formed from ash or lava.

VOYAGER A pair of U.S. space probes designed to provide detailed information about the outer regions of the solar system.

Voyager 1 was launched on September 5, 1977. Voyager 2 was launched on August 20, 1977, but traveled more slowly than Voyager 1. Both Voyagers are expected to remain operational until 2020, by which time they will be well outside the solar system.

WATER CYCLE The continuous cycling of water, as vapor, liquid, and solid, between the oceans, the atmosphere, and the land.

WATER VAPOR The gaseous form of water. Also sometimes referred to as moisture.

WEATHERING The breaking down of a rock, perhaps by water, ice, or repeated heating and cooling.

WHITE DWARF Any star originally of low mass that has reached the end of its life.

X-RAY An invisible form of radiation that has extremely short wavelengths just beyond the ultraviolet.

X-rays can go through many materials that light will not.

SET INDEX

Using the set index

This index covers all eight volumes in the *Space Science* set:

Vol. no. Title
1:   *How the universe works*
2:   *Sun and solar system*
3:   *Earth and Moon*
4:   *Rocky planets*
5:   *Gas giants*
6:   *Journey into space*
7:   *Shuttle to Space Station*
8:   *What satellites see*

An example entry:
Index entries are listed alphabetically.

———————/——————

Moon rover **3:** 48–49, **6:** 51
——————————/——

Volume numbers are in bold and are followed by page references.
   In the example above, "Moon rover" appears in Volume 3: *Earth and Moon* on pages 48–49 and in Volume 6: *Journey into space* on page 51. Many terms are also covered separately in the Glossary on pages 58–64.
   See, see also, or *see under* refers to another entry where there will be additional relevant information.

A
absolute zero **4:** 46, **5:** 54, **7:** 57
accretion (buildup) disk **1:** 36, 37, 39
active galactic nucleus **1:** 36, 37.
   See also black holes
Adrastea (Jupiter moon) **5:** 34, 35
aerodynamic design, rockets **6:** 7, 16, 22, **7:** 17
Agena (rocket) **6:** 41
air resistance **6:** 6, 7, 22
Albor Tholus (Mars volcano) **4:** 41
Aldrin, Jr., E. "Buzz" **3:** 44, **6:** 50
Alpha Regio (Venus) **4:** 25
aluminum, Earth **3:** 39
Amalthea (Jupiter moon) **5:** 34, 35
amino acids **4:** 54
ammonia:
   gas giants **5:** 6
   rocky planets **5:** 6
   Saturn **5:** 39
   Uranus **5:** 49
   See also ammonia-ice
ammonia-ice:
   comets **4:** 54
   Jupiter **5:** 14, 15
   Neptune **5:** 6
   Saturn **5:** 39, 40
   Uranus **5:** 6
Andromeda Galaxy (M31) **1:** 11, 12, 40–41, 50
antenna (pl. antennae) **6:** 31, 40, 52, 53, 54, 55, **7:** 6, 7, 26, 33, 38, **8:** 8, 49, 51, 57
anticyclones **5:** 10, 14, **8:** 20
apogee **3:** 8, 14
Apollo (Moon mission) **3:** 2, 4–5, 16–17, 44–45, 47, 48–49, 51, 52, 54, **6:** 2, 6, 10, 20, 42–51, **7:** 4, 17, 33, 34, 35, 44. *See also* Saturn (launcher)

Apollo applications program.
   See Skylab (space station)
Aqua (satellite) **8:** 14–15, 42
argon:
   Earth **3:** 22
   Moon **3:** 44
Ariane (launcher) **6:** 20, **8:** 10
Ariel (Uranus moon) **5:** 50, 51
Aristarchus (Greek thinker) **1:** 6
Aristarchus (Moon crater) **3:** 50
Armstrong, Neil **6:** 49, 50
Arsia Mons (Mars volcano) **4:** 41
Ascraeus Mons (Mars volcano) **4:** 41
ash:
   Earth **3:** 32, 39, 41
   Mercury **4:** 19
   See also lava
asteroid belt **2:** 47, **4:** 48, 49–50, 57, **6:** 54. *See also* Kirkwood gaps
asteroids **1:** 5, **2:** 4, 46, 51, **4:** 5, 48–52
   collisions with **2:** 51, 53, **4:** 9, 10, 11, 50, 51, 52, **5:** 21
   comet origin **4:** 48
   composition **2:** 51, **4:** 10, 51
   description **4:** 10, 48
   formation **2:** 54, **4:** 11, 50, 51
   irregular **4:** 11, 51
   Mars' moons **4:** 49
   mass **2:** 49, **4:** 51
   meteorite from **4:** 6
   numbers of **4:** 49
   orbits **2:** 46, 47, 51, **4:** 10, 48, 49, 50–51, 52, **6:** 57
   rotation **4:** 51
   See also asteroid belt; Astraea; Ceres; Eros; Gaspra; Hygiea; Ida; Juno; Pallas; Vesta
asthenosphere:
   Earth **3:** 31, 34
   Moon **3:** 55
Astraea (asteroid) **4:** 48
astronauts:
   Apollo (Moon mission) **3:** 44, 45, **6:** 43, 44–45, 46, 47, 49, 50, 51
   endurance **7:** 46
   exercise **7:** 33, 35, 38, 39, 54
   Gemini **6:** 38–39, 41
   gravity, effect of **6:** 41, **7:** 9, 10, 22, **8:** 30
   living space **7:** 23, 33, 34, 39, 41, 45, 50, 53–54
   showering **7:** 34, 35
   space, effect of **7:** 53, 54, 55
   weight **3:** 42
   weightlessness **6:** 16, **7:** 42
   See also cosmonauts; extravehicular activity; manned spaceflight
astronomical unit (AU), definition **1:** 10
astronomy **1:** 42, **7:** 56–57, **8:** 15, 54
astrophysics laboratory (Mir) **7:** 38, 41
asynchronous orbit **8:** 13
Atlantis (Space Shuttle) **7:** 2, 23, 36–37, 40–41
Atlas (launcher) **6:** 19, 35
Atlas (Saturn moon) **5:** 40, 41, 45
atomic mass units **2:** 9
atomic structure **7:** 54
atomic weapons **6:** 18. *See also* ballistic missiles
atomic weight **1:** 14
atoms **1:** 6, 14, 16, 17, 23, 26, 30, 54, 56, **2:** 8, 9, 12, 16, 22, 40, 45, 56, 57, **3:** 24, **4:** 54, **5:** 24, **7:** 57. *See also* atomic structure
Aurora Australis **3:** 21

Aurora Borealis **3:** 21
auroras:
   Earth **2:** 15, 38, 44–45, **3:** 19, 20–21, 24
   Ganymede **5:** 32
   Jupiter **5:** 16
   Uranus **5:** 50

B
ballistic missiles (ICBMs) **6:** 16, 17, 18–19
Beta Regio (Venus) **4:** 25
Betelgeuse (star) **2:** 13, 14
Big Bang **1:** 54, 55, 56, **7:** 55, **8:** 57
binary stars **1:** 18, 26, 30, 36
black dwarf stars **1:** 21, 29, **2:** 11
black holes **1:** 2, 5, 33, 35–39, 45, **8:** 56, 57
blue giants **1:** 14, 17, 22–23, 36, 51, **2:** 12, **8:** 54
Bok globules **1:** 14
booster pods (Russian launchers) **6:** 18, 19
boosters. *See under* Space Shuttle
Borrelly (comet) **4:** 52
bow shock **2:** 40, 41, 42
Butterfly Nebula **1:** 26, **2:** 10

C
calcium:
   stars **1:** 30
   Sun **2:** 16
   universe **1:** 14, 16
Callisto (Galilean satellite) **2:** 55, **5:** 8, 18–19, 30, 33–34
Caloris Basin (Mercury) **4:** 17, 18
Calypso (Saturn moon) **5:** 40, 41
Canada **2:** 45, **3:** 35, **7:** 45, 49, **8:** 21, 25, 42
Candor Chasm (Mars) **4:** 39
carbon:
   Callisto **5:** 34
   comets **4:** 54
   Earth **3:** 5, 16
   interplanetary dust **4:** 10
   Space Shuttle tiles **7:** 28
   stars **1:** 19, 26, 29, **2:** 11
   Sun **2:** 11, 17
   Titan **5:** 42
carbon dioxide:
   comets **4:** 53
   Earth **3:** 22, 27, 30, **4:** 36
   Mars **4:** 34. *See also* carbon dioxide ice
   Venus **4:** 23, 24, 25
carbon dioxide ice (dry ice), Mars **4:** 31, 32, 33, 34
carbon monoxide, comets **4:** 53
Cassini, Giovanni **3:** 9
Cassini division **5:** 44, 46
Cassini-Huygens (probe) **5:** 37, **6:** 21, 56, 57
Cat's Eye Nebula **1:** 26–27
Centaur (launcher) **6:** 21, 56
center of gravity:
   binary stars **1:** 18
   Earth and Moon **3:** 8, 54
centrifugal forces:
   Earth **3:** 10, 18, **4:** 22
   Moon **3:** 10
   Neptune **5:** 53
   satellites **8:** 10
   Saturn **5:** 39
   science fiction **7:** 42
   spacecraft **7:** 10, 42
   Uranus **5:** 49
   Venus **4:** 22
ceramic tiles, heat protection on Space Shuttle **7:** 27–28
Ceres (asteroid) **4:** 10, 48, 51
Cernan, Gene **6:** 41
Challenger (Space Shuttle) **7:** 23, 26–27
Chamberlin, Chrowder **2:** 53
Charon (Pluto moon) **4:** 44, 46–47, 57

Chasma Borealis (Mars) **4:** 32
chromosphere **2:** 18, 22, 32, 33, 35
circumference:
   Earth **3:** 18
   Mars **4:** 41
COBE (satellite) **8:** 57
Columbia (Space Shuttle) **7:** 17, 23, 26
coma (comet) **2:** 51, **4:** 52, 53, 55
combustion chamber. *See* engines
Comet Borrelly **4:** 52
comets **1:** 5, **2:** 4, 46, 51–52, **4:** 5, 6, 8, 10, 47, 48, 53–55
   atmosphere **4:** 53
   collisions with **2:** 52, 53, **5:** 21
   coma **2:** 51, **4:** 52, 53, 55
   Comet Borrelly **4:** 52
   composition **2:** 51, **4:** 8, 10, 53, 54, **5:** 34
   gravitational field **4:** 54
   Halley's Comet **4:** 54, 55
   lifespan **4:** 55
   mass **2:** 14, 49
   nucleus **2:** 51, **4:** 52, 53, 54
   orbits **2:** 51, 52, **4:** 53, 54, 57
   radiation **4:** 53
   Shoemaker-Levy 9 **4:** 53
   tails **2:** 38, 51, **4:** 53, 54
   word origin **4:** 53
   See also Kuiper belt; Oort cloud; *and under* ammonia-ice; carbon; carbon dioxide; carbon monoxide; dust; hydrogen; ice, water; methane; methane-ice; nitrogen; oxygen; plasma; rock; sulfur; water vapor
complementary color **5:** 49, 53
condensation:
   dust formation **1:** 26
   planet and moon formation **2:** 49, 54, **4:** 5, 4, 6, 17, 18
   water vapor **3:** 23, 29, **4:** 8
conduction **3:** 23, 55
constellations **1:** 8–9
   Andromeda **1:** 9, 23, 40, 41
   Aquila **1:** 9, 30, **6:** 54
   Circinus **1:** 8, 37
   Crux (Southern Cross) **1:** 8
   Draco **1:** 8, 9, 26–27, 47
   Gemini **1:** 8, 28
   Hydra **1:** 8, 35
   Lyra **1:** 9, 12
   Monoceros **1:** 8, 26
   Orion **1:** 8, 9, 13, 17
   Pegasus **1:** 9, 12
   Sagittarius **1:** 9, 11, 17, 18, 25
   Serpens **1:** 8, 16
   Taurus **1:** 9, 13, **6:** 54
   Ursa Major (Great Bear) **1:** 8
   Virgo **1:** 8, 39
   Vulpecula **1:** 9, 13
continental drift **3:** 36–37
convection/convection currents:
   Earth **3:** 23, 29, 32–33, 36
   Ganymede **5:** 32
   Jupiter **5:** 12
   Mars **4:** 36
   Sun **2:** 22, 23, 26, 28
   Venus **4:** 29
convective zone **2:** 18–19, 22, 23
Cooper, Jr., Gordon **6:** 35, 37
Copernicus **1:** 6, **2:** 48
Cordelia (Uranus moon) **5:** 51
corona (pl. coronae) (star) **2:** 19, 22, 35–37, 38, 41, 53, **3:** 15
corona (pl. coronae) (Venus) **4:** 27
coronal loops **2:** 35, 36–37. *See also* prominences
coronal mass ejections **2:** 4–5, 22–23, 35, 44
Cosmic Background Explorer (COBE) **8:** 57
Cosmological Principle **1:** 42, 49
cosmonauts **6:** 31, 32–33, 35, 39, **7:** 30, 32, 39, 41, 46, **8:** 30

Cosmonaut Training Center 6: 33
cosmos 1: 4, 5, 38, 42, 50, 3: 5
Crab Nebula 1: 12, 13, 21, 32–33, 34
Crater Mound. See Meteor Crater
craters:
  Callisto 5: 33, 34
  Dione 5: 42
  Earth 4: 9, 52, 57
  Ganymede 5: 30, 32
  Mars 4: 38, 40, 41
  Mercury 4: 9, 14, 16, 18, 19
  Mimas (Herschel Crater) 5: 42
  Moon 2: 51, 3: 42, 45, 46, 47,
    50–51, 52, 55, 56, 57, 4: 9
  Neptune's irregular moons 5: 56
  Oberon 5: 51
  Phobos 4: 42
  Pluto 4: 45
  Tethys 5: 42
  Umbriel 5: 51
  Venus 4: 25, 28, 29
  See also Aristarchus (Moon
    crater), Cunitz Crater
    (Venus); Daedalus (Moon
    crater); Leonov Crater
    (Moon); Meteor Crater;
    rays, crater
crescent Moon 3: 13. See also
  phases
Crux (constellation) 1: 8
Cunitz, Maria 4: 28
Cunitz Crater (Venus) 4: 28
cyclones 3: 26, 5: 10, 8: 23
  tropical cyclones 8: 22
  See also hurricanes

D
Daedalus (Moon crater) 3: 51
dark matter 1: 5, 40
deep space network (NASA) 2: 20
Deimos (Mars moon) 4: 42
Delta (launcher) 8: 12–13
deorbit 7: 32, 35
depressions (weather) 8: 20, 21,
  22, 25
deserts:
  Earth 3: 36, 40, 4: 38, 8: 38,
    43, 46
  Mars 4: 38
DG Tau (star) 1: 48
"diamond ring" (Sun) 3: 14–15
diffraction 3: 44
dinosaurs, extinction of 2: 51, 4: 52
Dione (Saturn moon) 5: 36, 40, 42,
  43, 45
Discoverer (satellite) 6: 26, 27
Discovery (Space Shuttle) 7: 16,
  23, 51
docking, spacecraft 6: 2, 3, 38, 40,
  41, 44, 45, 46, 49, 7: 13, 30,
  32, 33, 34, 36–37, 38, 41, 44,
  46, 52, 53
dog (Laika), first living creature
  in space 6: 23
Doppler effect 6: 23
"double planet" 3: 18, 4: 46
drag 7: 9
Dreyer, John Ludvig Emil 1: 12
dry ice. See carbon dioxide ice
Dumbbell Nebula 1: 13
dust 1: 4, 14, 17, 20, 26, 29, 36, 40,
  45, 2: 8, 4: 54, 8: 54
  comets 2: 52, 53, 4: 52, 53
  Earth 2: 53, 8: 4–5
  Mars 4: 34
  Moon 3: 44
  solar system origin 2: 53, 54
  See also gas and dust clouds;
    interplanetary dust;
    interstellar matter
dust storms, Mars 4: 33, 34, 35,
  36–37
dwarf stars 1: 19, 22, 2: 6, 10, 12.
  See also black dwarf stars;
  white dwarf stars

E
"Eagle." See lunar module
Eagle Nebula 1: 16
Earth 2: 46, 47, 48, 50, 55, 3: 16–41,
  4: 4, 5
  atmosphere 2: 9, 23, 26, 41, 3: 5,
    6–7, 22–27, 30, 36, 39, 45,
    52, 6: 8, 11, 23, 25, 7: 6–7,
    41, 56, 8: 8, 20–27, 41. See
    also exosphere; ionosphere;
    mesosphere; stratosphere;
    thermosphere; troposphere
  atmospheric pressure 4: 23
  auroras 2: 15, 38, 44–45,
    3: 19, 20–21, 24
  "greenhouse" effect 4: 36
  sky, color of 3: 44
  storms 3: 26, 8: 23, 25
  weather patterns 8: 19, 20–27
  winds 3: 29, 40, 8: 43
  axis 2: 14, 3: 8, 11, 16, 18
  centrifugal forces 3: 10, 18, 4: 22
  circumference 3: 18
  death 2: 10
  density 3: 19
  energy 3: 29, 32, 39
  formation 3: 30, 39
  gravity/gravitational field
    3: 8, 10, 18, 6: 8, 51, 7: 10,
    8: 18–19
    Earth and Moon center of
      gravity 3: 8, 54
    escaping from 6: 6, 8, 9, 22,
      33, 7: 9, 10, 8: 10, 13
    formation 3: 30
    simulation 7: 42, 56
  heat 3: 22, 23, 27, 29, 30, 32, 39
  inside:
    asthenosphere 3: 31, 34
    convection currents 3: 23, 29,
      32–33, 36
    core 3: 19, 31, 38, 39
    crust 3: 19, 30–35, 36–37, 38,
      39, 40, 41, 4: 51
    lithosphere 3: 30, 31
    mantle 3: 30, 31, 34, 38,
      39, 40
    plates 3: 30–37, 39, 41
  magnetism/magnetic field 2: 42,
    45, 3: 19–21, 24, 38, 5: 16,
    6: 26, 7: 56, 8: 56. See also
    magnetosphere
  magnetosphere 2: 38, 42, 44, 45,
    3: 20–21, 24
  Mars, Earth seen from 3: 6
  mass 2: 53, 3: 19, 39
  Moon. see Moon
  orbit 2: 47, 3: 8, 10, 11, 16, 18,
    4: 7, 22, 6: 56, 57
  pressure 2: 16, 3: 38, 39, 42
  radiation 4: 36, 8: 26, 57. See
    also Van Allen belts
  radioactive decay 3: 32, 39
  radio waves 2: 41, 3: 22, 6: 23
  radius 3: 18
  rotation 2: 14, 7: 13
  seasons 3: 10–11, 8: 19
  shape and size 3: 5, 16, 18–19,
    4: 5
  surface area 3: 19
  surface features. See glaciers;
    and under ash; craters;
    deserts; erosion; faults/
    fractures; flooding; ice
    caps; lava/lava flows;
    magma; mountains/
    mountain ranges; oceans;
    rifts/rift valleys;
    sand dunes; "soils";
    volcanoes/volcanic activity
  temperature 3: 27, 28, 39, 8: 27
  tilt 3: 8, 11, 16
  See also aluminum;
    earthquakes; surveying
    (and mapping) Earth; and
    under argon; carbon;

Earth (continued...)
  carbon dioxide; dust;
  helium; hydrogen;
  ice, water; iron; light;
  magnesium; meteorites;
  meteoroids; nitrogen;
  oxygen; phases; reflect,
  ability to; rock; silicate
  minerals; silicon; snow;
  sulfur; tides; ultraviolet
  radiation; water; water
  vapor
earthquakes 2: 16, 32, 3: 32, 33,
  38, 8: 46
eccentric orbits:
  Moon 3: 9
  Nereid 5: 56
  Pluto 4: 44
Echo (satellite) 6: 28, 8: 8
eclipses 2: 14, 32, 33, 47, 3: 9, 14–15
ecliptic plane 2: 47
EGGs (evaporating gaseous
  globules) 1: 16
Einstein, Albert 1: 46, 48, 2: 9
electronics 6: 27, 7: 6, 8: 19, 20
electrons 1: 34, 36, 39, 2: 8, 9, 32,
  41, 42, 45, 3: 19
elements. See individual entries
El Niño 8: 20
Elysium Mons (Mars volcano) 4: 41
Enceladus (Saturn moon) 5: 6–7, 36,
  40, 42, 44
Encke gap (Saturn rings) 5: 44, 46
Endeavour (Space Shuttle) 7: 23, 51
energy:
  Big Bang 1: 54
  Earth 3: 29, 32, 39
  galaxies 1: 40, 2: 8
  Io 5: 22
  Jupiter 5: 8, 15
  meteor impact 4: 57
  quasars 1: 35
  relativity, theory of 1: 46, 48, 2: 9
  stars 1: 21, 23, 26, 30, 31, 35, 45
  Sun 2: 8–9, 16, 21, 22, 28, 31, 32,
    33, 38, 46, 3: 22, 28, 8: 26
  universe 1: 4
  Uranus 5: 50
engines (launcher and spacecraft)
  6: 10, 11–13, 16, 19, 8: 14
  catalysts 7: 18, 20
  combustion chamber 6: 12, 13,
    7: 20
  cryogenic 6: 20
  Goddard's double acting 6: 14
  gravity, overcoming 7: 9, 10, 13
  hypergolic 6: 11, 7: 20
  lunar module 6: 46, 47
  Mir 7: 38, 39
  oxidizers 6: 11, 12, 13, 16
  reaction 6, 6: 12–13, 7: 20
  Skylab 7: 34
  Space Shuttle 6: 13, 7: 14, 15, 18,
    20, 21, 23, 27
    inertial upper stage 7: 25
  Titan 6: 56
  See also fuel; propulsion
    systems; takeoffs; thrusters
Enterprise (Space Shuttle) 7: 17, 23
Eros (asteroid) 4: 50
erosion:
  Callisto 5: 33
  Earth 3: 23, 28, 29, 34, 38, 40,
    41, 8: 44
  Mars 4: 40
  Moon 3: 49, 50
ERTS-1 (satellite) 8: 28–29, 34.
  See also Landsat
ESA (European Space Agency) 6: 20,
  7: 49, 8: 7, 10
Eskimo Nebula 1: 28, 2: 11
Eta Carinae (nebula) 1: 10
EUE (Extreme Ultraviolet Explorer)
  8: 57
Europa (Galilean satellite) 2: 50, 55,
  5: 8, 16, 18–19, 26, 28–29, 34

Europe 3: 34, 37, 6: 20, 28, 7: 45
European Space Agency. See ESA
European space initiatives. See
  Ariane; ESA; International
  Space Station; Meteosat
EVA. See extravehicular activity
evaporation:
  dry ice 4: 34
  star formation 1: 16
  Sun death 2: 10
  water cycle 3: 28, 29
exosphere 3: 22
expanding universe 1: 42, 53–57
experiments in space 6: 33, 50,
  7: 24, 26, 41, 49, 54–57.
  See also laboratories in space
Explorer (satellite) 6: 17, 24–25,
  8: 8, 28, 56
external tank. See under Space
  Shuttle
extinction, dinosaur 2: 51, 4: 52
extravehicular activity (EVA)
  (spacewalking) 6: 38–39, 41,
  50, 51, 7: 36, 41, 44, 46–47
Extreme Ultraviolet Explorer (EUE)
  8: 57

F
Faith 7 (Mercury mission) 6: 37
false-color images, explained
  8: 25, 34
faults/fractures:
  Dione 5: 42
  Earth 3: 33, 8: 37, 46
  Mercury 4: 17, 18
  Venus 4: 26–27, 28
  See also corona (Venus); nova
    (Venus); rifts/rift valleys
filters 2: 32, 33. See also
  multispectral images
flares 2: 19, 24, 32–33, 35, 45
flight paths 6: 56, 57, 7: 10–11, 20.
  See also orbits; trajectory
flooding:
  Earth 8: 23, 25, 30, 38
  Mars 4: 31
fractures. See faults/fractures
Freedom 7 (Mercury mission) 6: 34
friction 3: 9, 6: 8, 7: 10, 27. See also
  air resistance
Friendship 7 (Mercury mission)
  6: 34, 35, 36, 37
fuel, spacecraft 6: 7, 8, 9, 10, 11,
  12, 13, 14, 16, 19, 20, 31, 44,
  46, 52, 56, 7: 9, 13, 14, 18,
  19, 20. See also propellants
full Moon 3: 9, 12, 13, 47. See also
  phases
fusion 1: 18, 20, 2: 8, 9, 10, 21

G
G2V star (Sun) 2: 12
Gagarin, Yuri 6: 32–33
galaxies 1: 4, 40–45, 2: 6, 8: 56, 57
  cataloguing 1: 12
  definition 1: 40
  formation 1: 42, 54, 55, 56
  gravity/gravitational field 1: 42,
    47, 56
  mass 1: 24, 40
  size 1: 11
  star rotation 1: 42
  types 1: 42–43, 45
    elliptical 1: 19, 23, 39, 42, 43,
      45, 46–47, 50
    irregular 1: 18, 42, 43, 45, 51
    radio 1: 45
    spiral 1: 19, 30, 40, 42, 43, 45,
      46–47, 50, 52–53, 2: 6
  See also Andromeda Galaxy;
    Big Bang; Hubble's Law;
    Local Group; Magellanic
    Clouds; Milky Way Galaxy;
    and under energy; helium;
    hydrogen; light; reflect,
    ability to; X-rays

Galilean satellites **5:** 18, 19–34.
See also Callisto; Europa;
Ganymede; Io
Galilei, Galileo **1:** 6, **2:** 48, **5:** 18
Galileo (probe) **3:** 42, **4:** 20, **5:** 9,
10, 12–13, 18, 21, 23, **6:** 56, 57
gamma rays **2:** 21, 33
Ganymede (Galilean satellite)
2: 55, **5:** 6, 8, 16, 18–19, 26,
30–32, 34
gas, interstellar **1:** 4, 14, 16, 17,
19, 20, 26, 28, 29, 36, 37, 39,
40, 56, **2:** 8, **8:** 54. See also gas
and dust clouds; ionized gas
gas and dust clouds **1:** 14, 17–18,
19, 20, 23, 26–27, 30–31, 33,
42, **2:** 8, 53, 54, **3:** 56. See also
nebula
gas giant moons **2:** 50, 57, **5:** 6–7.
See also Galilean satellites;
and under Jupiter; Neptune;
Saturn; Uranus
gas giants **2:** 50, **5:** 4 and
throughout
formation **2:** 56–57, **5:** 4, 6, 17,
18, 48, 49, 50
ring formation **5:** 7, 34, 35,
45, 46
See also Jupiter; Neptune;
Saturn; Uranus
gas plumes:
Io **5:** 23, 25
Neptune (geysers) **5:** 56
Gaspra (asteroid) **4:** 10, **6:** 57
geiger tubes **6:** 24
Gemini (spacecraft) **6:** 2, 3, 38–41
George C. Marshall Space Flight
Center **6:** 17
geostationary orbit **7:** 5, 25, **8:** 13
geostationary satellites **6:** 28, **8:** 7,
14, 23, 26. See also global
positioning system
geosynchronous orbit **7:** 10, 12–13,
8: 13, 14–15, 19, 23
geosynchronous satellites **7:** 12, 13
German Rocket Society **6:** 16
Germany **6:** 14, 16
geysers, on Triton **5:** 56
gibbous Moon **3:** 12, 13. See also
phases
gimbals **6:** 12, 13, 16, **7:** 20, 25
glaciers **2:** 32, **3:** 28, **8:** 30, 31, 38
glass:
fiber **7:** 28
Moon rock **3:** 52
"stardust" **4:** 10
Glenn, John **6:** 34, 35
global positioning system (GPS)
6: 23, **7:** 5, **8:** 4, 7, 13, 14
Goddard, Robert **6:** 14–16, 17
GOES (satellite) **8:** 17, 23–26
Grace (satellite) **8:** 18–19
granulation **2:** 24, 26, 27, 28
gravity/gravitational field:
"assists" (slingshot) **4:** 14, 54,
6: 52, 55, 56
asteroids **4:** 10, 11, 51
astronauts **6:** 41, **7:** 9, 10, 22,
8: 30
Big Bang **1:** 56
black holes **1:** 33, 36
Callisto **5:** 34
comets: **4:** 54
cosmos **1:** 5
craters **3:** 51
Earth **3:** 8, 10, 18, **6:** 8, 51, **7:** 10,
8: 18–19
escaping from **6:** 8, 9, 22,
33, **7:** 9, 10, **8:** 10, 13
formation **3:** 30
simulation **7:** 42, 56
Europa **5:** 34
experiments (ISS) **7:** 54–57
galaxies **1:** 42, 47, 56
Ganymede **5:** 34
Io **5:** 22, 34

gravity (continued...)
Jupiter **4:** 49, **5:** 6, 8, 17, 22, 34
light, effect on **1:** 46, 47
Mars and its moons **4:** 30, 33, 42
Mercury **4:** 12, 15
Moon **3:** 8, 10, 42, 44, 51, 54
Neptune **5:** 5, 56
pull (g) **7:** 9, 22
Saturn **5:** 6, 39, 45, 46
solar system origin **2:** 53, 54, 57
sphere-making **4:** 11, **5:** 34, 56
stars **1:** 18, 19, 20, 23, 24, 26, 29,
30, 31, 42, 56, **2:** 8, 9
Sun **2:** 8, 9, 14, 16, 46, **3:** 10,
8: 56
understanding **7:** 57
universe, all objects in **3:** 18
Uranus **5:** 49, 50
variance **8:** 18–19
See also center of gravity; laws
of motion; Newton, Sir
Isaac; theory of relativity
Great Bear **1:** 8
Great Dark Spot (Neptune) **5:** 54
Great Red Spot (Jupiter) **5:** 4–5,
10, 14, 15
"greenhouse" effect:
Earth **4:** 36
Venus **4:** 24–25
ground station **6:** 28, 31, **7:** 6,
8: 8, 9, 13, 14
Gula Mons (Venus) **4:** 28
gyroscopes **6:** 12, 16

H
half Moon **3:** 12, 13. See also
phases
Halley, Sir Edmund **4:** 55
Halley's Comet **4:** 54, 55
heat shields **5:** 12, **6:** 26, 33, 40, 44,
46, 51, **7:** 27, **8:** 57
Hecates Tholus (Mars volcano)
Helene (Saturn moon) **5:** 40, 41
heliopause **2:** 40, 41
helioseismology **2:** 16, 32
heliosphere (Sun) **2:** 40–41, 44, 45
heliotail **2:** 40
helium:
Big Bang **1:** 54
Earth **3:** 22
galaxies **1:** 42
gas giants **2:** 50, **5:** 6
Jupiter **5:** 6, 15, 17
Mercury **4:** 14, 16
Moon **3:** 44
Neptune **5:** 6, 53
Saturn **5:** 6, 39
space **2:** 56–57
stars **1:** 14, 21, 23, 24, 26, 28,
29, 42
Sun **2:** 8–9, 11, 17, 21, 22, 40
universe **1:** 14
Uranus **5:** 6, 48, 49
word origin **2:** 17
Hellas Basin (Mars) **4:** 41
Heracleides (Greek thinker) **1:** 6
Herschel, William and John **1:** 7, 12
Herschel Crater (Mimas) **5:** 42
Hertzsprung, Ejnor **2:** 10
Hertzsprung-Russell diagram **2:** 11
Hubble, Edwin Powell **1:** 42–43,
45, 53
Hubble Space Telescope **7:** 2, 5, 17,
56, **8:** 2, 54, 56–57
how Hubble "sees" **1:** 7
images taken by **1:** 7 and
throughout, **4:** 30, 31,
32–33, 44, 45; **5:** 16,
8: 54, 55
Hubble's Law **1:** 42, 53
Hubble-V (gas cloud) **1:** 18
hurricanes **3:** 26, **7:** 57, **8:** 20, 22,
23, 25, 26
Huygens gap (Saturn rings) **5:** 46
Huygens (probe) **6:** 21, 57. See also
Cassini-Huygens

hydrazine **6:** 11, **7:** 20
hydrogen:
Big Bang **1:** 54
comets **4:** 54
Earth **3:** 22
galaxies **1:** 45
gas giants **2:** 50, 56–57, **5:** 6
interstellar wind **2:** 40
Jupiter **5:** 6, 15, 17
Lagoon Nebula **1:** 11
Mercury **4:** 16
Moon **3:** 44
Neptune **5:** 6, 53
rocky planets **2:** 56–57
Saturn **5:** 6, 38, 39
spacecraft fuel (liquid
hydrogen) **6:** 11, 56, **7:** 14,
15, 18, 20, 21
stars **1:** 14, 16, 17, 20, 21, 23, 24,
26, 28, 29, 42, 45
Sun **2:** 8–9, 10, 12, 17, 21, 22, 40
universe **1:** 14
Uranus **5:** 6, 48, 49
Hygiea (asteroid) **4:** 51
Hyperion (Saturn moon) **5:** 41, 45

I
Iapetus (Saturn moon) **5:** 41, 42,
43, 45
ICBMs (intercontinental ballistic
missiles). See ballistic missiles
ice, water
Callisto **5:** 30, 33, 34
Charon **4:** 46
comets **2:** 46, 51, **4:** 54
condensation **4:** 8
Earth **3:** 6, 22, 28, **8:** 25, 30,
38, 41
Europa **2:** 50, **5:** 19, 28–29
Ganymede **5:** 30, 32
gas giant rings **5:** 6
gas giants **5:** 4
Iapetus **5:** 42
Kuiper belt **4:** 47
Mars **4:** 31, 34, 35
Neptune **5:** 6, 55
Pluto **4:** 8, 44
Saturn/Saturn's rings **5:** 38,
40, 45
solar system origin **2:** 56–57
Tethys **5:** 42
Triton **5:** 56
Uranus/Uranus' moons **5:** 6, 49,
50, 51
See also ammonia-ice; carbon
dioxide ice (dry ice);
ice caps; methane-ice;
nitrogen-ice
ice caps:
Earth **3:** 28, **4:** 32
Mars **4:** 31, 32–33, 34, 36
Mercury **4:** 17
See also polar caps
Ida (asteroid) **4:** 51, **6:** 57
inertial upper stage (IUS) **7:** 25
inflation **1:** 54, 55. See also
expanding universe
infrared:
false-color images **8:** 34–35, 37
satellites **6:** 27, **8:** 8, 22, 24, 25,
26, 44, 56, 57
stars **1:** 17, 18, **8:** 57
Sun, light energy from **2:** 9
thermal imaging **8:** 41
Infrared Astronomical Satellite
(IRAS) **8:** 57
inner planets. See Mercury; Venus;
Earth; Mars
INTELSAT VI (satellite) **8:** 10–11
interferogram **8:** 51
interferometry **8:** 51
International Space Station (ISS)
7: 16, 41, 42–57, **8:** 4
crew **7:** 52, 53–54
modules:
Destiny lab **7:** 45, 52

International Space Station (ISS)
(continued...)
emergency crew vehicle
(X-38) **7:** 44, 53
laboratory **7:** 49, 52, 54–57
Leonardo **7:** 45, 52
Pirs **7:** 44, 52, 53
Raffaello **7:** 52
remote manipulator system
(RMS) **7:** 45, 46–47,
49, 52
solar panels **7:** 42, 45
trusses **7:** 45, 52, 53
Unity **7:** 42–43, 45, 50, 51, 52
Zarya **7:** 42–43, 45, 50, 51, 52
Zvezda **7:** 44, 52
orbit **7:** 46
Freedom, former name **7:** 44
living space **7:** 53–54
Mir, learning from **7:** 46
pictures taken from **8:** 30, 31
interplanetary dust **4:** 10, 11. See
also dust; interstellar matter;
micrometeorites
interstellar gas. See gas, interstellar
interstellar matter **1:** 14, 23, 40,
2: 40, 41. See also dust; gas,
interstellar; interplanetary
dust; micrometeorites
Io (Galilean satellite) **2:** 50, 55,
5: 8, 16, 18, 19, 20–26, 34
ionization **2:** 8
ionized gas **1:** 17, **2:** 26, 33, 35, 46.
See also plasma
ionized particles **3:** 24, **5:** 26.
See also auroras; plasma;
prominences; spicules
ionosphere **2:** 41, 45, **3:** 21, 22, 24,
6: 23
IRAS (Infrared Astronomical
Satellite) **8:** 57
iron:
Earth **3:** 19, 39
Europa **5:** 29
Io **5:** 26
Mars **4:** 31, 43
Mercury **4:** 12, 17, 19
meteorites **4:** 6, 57
Moon **3:** 52, 56
oxide (catalyst) **7:** 18
rocky planets **4:** 8
stars **1:** 19, 30, 31
Sun **2:** 17
isotopes, radioactive.
See radioisotopes
Italy **7:** 45, 52, **8:** 31

J
Janus (Saturn moon) **5:** 40, 44, 46
Japan **7:** 45, 49, **8:** 37
Jeans, Sir James **2:** 53
Jeffreys, Sir Harold **2:** 53
Jovian planets **3:** 6, **4:** 8, **5:** 4, 6.
See also gas giants
Juno (asteroid) **4:** 48
Jupiter (launcher) **6:** 19, 24
Jupiter (planet) **2:** 46, 47, 49, 50,
55, **4:** 4, 48, 49, 57, **5:** 2, 4, 5, 6,
8–18, **6:** 52, 54, 55, 56, 57
atmosphere **5:** 9, 10–15
anticyclones **5:** 10, 14
atmospheric pressure **5:** 12
auroras **5:** 16
clouds **5:** 10–11, 14–15
convection currents **5:** 12
storms **5:** 14
weather patterns **5:** 10–15
winds **5:** 14
axis **5:** 9
composition **5:** 4, 6, 8, 9, 15,
16–17
density **5:** 8
direction **5:** 4, 8
formation **2:** 56–57, **5:** 4–5,
17, 18
gravity **4:** 49, **5:** 6, 8, 17, 22, 34

Jupiter (*continued...*)
Great Red Spot **5:** 4–5, 10, 14, 15
heat **5:** 8, 12, 16, 17
magnetism/magnetic field **5:** 8, 15–16, 26, **6:** 54, 55
magnetosphere **5:** 15, 32
mass **2:** 49, **5:** 8, 17
moons **5:** 6–7, 8, 9, 15, 16, 18–35. *See also* Galilean satellites
orbit **2:** 47, **5:** 4, **6:** 56, 57
pressure **5:** 17
probes. *See* Galileo; Pioneer; Voyager
radiation **5:** 15
radio waves **5:** 8, 15
rings **5:** 6, 7, 8, 34, 35
rotation **5:** 9, 35
shape and size **5:** 5, 8
star, potential to be **5:** 8, 17
temperature **5:** 11, 12, 16, 17
See also Shoemaker-Levy 9; *and under* ammonia-ice; energy; helium; hydrogen; metallic hydrogen; methane; phosphorous; polar caps; rock; sulfur; water

K
Kant, Immanuel **2:** 53, 54
"Kaputnik" **6:** 24
Keeler gap (Saturn rings) **5:** 46
Kennedy, President John F. **6:** 17, 38
Kennedy Space Center **6:** 4, 19, **7:** 20
Kepler, Johannes **1:** 6, **2:** 48, **3:** 9
kerosene **6:** 11, 19
kiloparsec, definition **1:** 11
Kirkwood gaps (asteroid belt) **4:** 49
Kuiper belt **2:** 51, 52, **4:** 47, 57

L
laboratories in space:
International Space Station (ISS) **7:** 49, 52, 54–57
Mir **7:** 38, 41
Space Shuttle **7:** 24, 26
Lagoon Nebula **1:** 11
Laika, the dog (first living creature in space) **6:** 23
Landsat **8:** 14, 34–39, 45
landslides, Mars **4:** 41
La Niña **8:** 20
Laplace, Pierre-Simon **2:** 53
launchers/launch vehicles **6:** 4–5, 9–13, 14–21, 22, 24, 38, 43, 52, 56, **7:** 34, 46, **8:** 10. *See also* Ariane (launcher); Atlas (launcher); engines; Jupiter (launcher); propellants; propulsion systems; retrorockets; rocketry; rockets; Saturn (launcher); takeoffs; Thor (launcher); thrusters; Titan (launcher); Vanguard (launcher)
lava/lava flows:
Dione **5:** 42
Earth **3:** 29, 32, 38, 39, 41
Io **5:** 21, 22, 23, 25–26
Mars **4:** 40, 43
Mercury **4:** 17, 18, 19
Moon **3:** 42, 46, 47, 48–49, 52, 54, 55, 56
Venus **4:** 25, 26, 27, 28, 29
laws of motion **1:** 6, **2:** 38, 53, **6:** 12, 41
Leonov Crater (Moon) **3:** 47
life:
development **1:** 50, **2:** 9, 46, **3:** 5, 16, 22, 27, 30, **4:** 54
evidence of on other planets/moons **1:** 48, **5:** 29
extinction **2:** 10, 51, **3:** 19, **4:** 52
first human being in space **6:** 33

life (*continued...*)
first living creature in space **6:** 23, 30
identifying life on Earth from space **3:** 6–7
lift/lifting force. *See under* rockets
liftoffs. *See* takeoffs
light:
Big Bang **1:** 55, 56
black hole **1:** 36
Earth **2:** 6, **3:** 13
blue sky **3:** 44
galaxies **1:** 40, 45, 50, 53
Ganymede **5:** 30
gravity, effect of **1:** 46, 47
Mars **4:** 31, 36
Moon **3:** 13, 47
Neptune **5:** 53
quasars **1:** 35
rays of **1:** 36
speed of **1:** 10
stars **1:** 16, 18, 24, 29, 30, 33, 39, 42, 45
Sun **2:** 6, 9, 11, 16–17, 21, 23, 24, 32, 41, 46, **3:** 11, 13, 14–15, 22
elements within **2:** 16–17
time machine **1:** 50, 53
universe **1:** 7
visible **1:** 5, 18, 30, **2:** 9, 21, 32, **4:** 20, **8:** 22, 24, 33, 34, 38
See also complementary color; filters; infrared; light-year; photons; radiation; ultraviolet light; X-rays
light-year, definition **1:** 10–11
lithosphere:
Earth **3:** 30, 31
Moon **3:** 55
Local Group **1:** 50, **2:** 7
lunar eclipse **3:** 14
lunar module (LM) ("Eagle") **6:** 20, 43, 44, 45, 46, 47, 48, 49, 50. *See also* Apollo (Moon mission)

M
megaparsec, definition **1:** 11
Magellan, Ferdinand **1:** 51, **4:** 25
Magellan (probe) **4:** 25
Magellanic Clouds **1:** 11, 45, 50, 51, **2:** 7, **8:** 54
magma:
Earth **3:** 32, 33, 38, 40
Venus **4:** 26
See also lava/lava flows
magnesium:
Earth **3:** 39
Sun **2:** 17
magnetism/magnetic field:
black holes **1:** 2, 39
cosmos **1:** 5
Earth **2:** 42, 45, **3:** 19–21, 24, 38, **5:** 16, **6:** 26, **7:** 56, **8:** 56
Ganymede **5:** 32
Io **5:** 15, 16
Jupiter **5:** 8, 15–16, 26, **6:** 54, 55
Mercury **4:** 19
Moon **3:** 55
Neptune **5:** 55, **6:** 55
Saturn **5:** 37, 38, **6:** 55
Sun/sunspots **2:** 16, 28, 32, 33, 35, 37, 41, 42–45, 46
supernova **1:** 29
Uranus **5:** 49, 50, **6:** 55
See also magnetopause; magnetospheres
magnetopause **2:** 42
magnetospheres:
Earth **2:** 38, 42, 44, 45, **3:** 20–21, 24
Ganymede **5:** 32
Jupiter **5:** 15, 32
Sun's heliosphere **2:** 40–41
See also magnetopause; magnetotail

magnetotail **3:** 21
magnitude, star **2:** 13, **8:** 56
main-sequence stars **1:** 18, 24, 30, **2:** 9, 10, 12
man, first in space **6:** 32–33
manned spaceflight **3:** 6, **6:** 6, 9, 24, 26, 30–51, 52, **8:** 30. *See also* Apollo; Gemini; Soyuz; Space Shuttle
mare (pl. maria) **3:** 42, 43, 46, 47, 52, 54, 55, **4:** 17, 31, 38
Mariner (probe) **4:** 12, 14, 15, 16, **6:** 52, 53
Mars **2:** 42, 46, 47, 48, 50, 55, **4:** 2, 4, 5, 6, 30–43, **6:** 52
atmosphere **4:** 33–37
clouds **4:** 31, 32, 34, 35
convection **4:** 36
dust storms **4:** 33, 34, 35, 36–37
weather patterns **4:** 34
winds **4:** 33, 36, 38
axis **4:** 32
circumference **4:** 41
color **4:** 30, 31
density **4:** 43
formation **4:** 43
gravity **4:** 30, 33, 42
heat **4:** 36, 43
inside:
core **4:** 43
crust **4:** 41, 43
mantle **4:** 43
plates **4:** 41
mass **4:** 30
moons **4:** 42
orbit **2:** 47, **4:** 7, 31, 32, 50
pressure **4:** 34
probes. *See* Mars Global Surveyor; Viking mission
radiation **4:** 36
radioactive decay **4:** 43
radius **4:** 43
rotation **4:** 31, 32
seasons **4:** 32
shape and size **4:** 5, 30
surface features:
basins **4:** 41
"canals" **4:** 38
chasm **4:** 32, 39
craters **4:** 38, 40, 41
deserts **4:** 38
erosion **4:** 40
flooding **4:** 31
gullies **4:** 40
highlands **4:** 38
ice caps **4:** 31, 32–33, 34, 36
landslides **4:** 41
lava/lava flows **4:** 40, 43
mare (pl. maria) **4:** 38
plains **4:** 40, 41
polar caps **4:** 31, 34
ridges **4:** 38
rift valleys **4:** 41
sand dunes **4:** 36
"soils" **4:** 34, 43
volcanoes **4:** 38, 40, 41, 43
temperature **4:** 34, 36
tilt **4:** 32
See also noble gases; *and under* carbon dioxide; carbon dioxide ice (dry ice); dust; ice, water; iron; light; nitrogen; oxygen; reflect, ability to; rock; water; water vapor
Mars Global Surveyor (probe) **4:** 30
mascons (Moon) **3:** 54, 55
mathematics, laws of **1:** 6
matter, conversion into energy by:
galaxies **1:** 40
Sun **1:** 23, **2:** 9, 21, 22
Maxwell gap (Saturn rings) **5:** 46
Maxwell Montes (Venus) **4:** 25, 26
measurements in space **1:** 10–11
Melas Chasm (Mars) **4:** 39

magnetotail **3:** 21
Mercury (planet) **1:** 6, 9, **2:** 46, 47, 48, 50, 55, **4:** 4, 5, 6, 7, 9, 12–19, **6:** 52
atmosphere **4:** 14, 15–17
axis **4:** 15
death **2:** 10
density **4:** 12
gravity/gravitational field **4:** 12, 15
heat **4:** 16
inside:
core **4:** 12, 19
crust **4:** 12, 16, 18, 19
mantle **4:** 19
magnetic field **4:** 19
orbit **2:** 47, **4:** 7, 12, 14, 15, 16
probes. *See* Mariner (probe)
radioactive decay **4:** 43
rotation **4:** 15
shape and size **4:** 5, 12, 14, 19
surface features **4:** 17–19
basins **4:** 17, 18
craters **4:** 9, 14, 16, 18, 19
depressions **4:** 18
faults/fractures **4:** 17, 18
ice caps **4:** 17
lava/lava flows **4:** 17, 18, 19
mare (pl. maria) **4:** 17
mountains **4:** 16, 17, 18
plains **4:** 16, 19
ridges **4:** 16, 17, 19
scarps (escarpments) **4:** 16, 18
"soils" **4:** 17, 18
valleys **4:** 16
temperature **4:** 16
See also under ash; helium; hydrogen; iron; oxygen; phases; potassium; reflect, ability to; sodium; titanium
Mercury (spacecraft) **6:** 30, 34–37. *See also* Faith 7; Freedom 7; Friendship 7
mesosphere **3:** 22, 24
messages, from Earth into space **6:** 54
Messier, Charles **1:** 12
Messier Catalogue **1:** 12, 13, 33
metallic hydrogen:
Jupiter **5:** 17
Saturn **5:** 38
Meteor Crater, Arizona **4:** 9, 52
meteorites **4:** 6, 55–57
age **4:** 11
analysis **2:** 52, 57, **7:** 57
asteroid origin **4:** 57
Big Bang **1:** 54
definition **4:** 11, 55
Earth, collisions **2:** 57, **3:** 30, 45, **4:** 52, 55, 57
images of **4:** 6, 11, 38
Mars, collisions **4:** 57
Mercury, collisions **4:** 18, 19
Moon, collisions **3:** 45, 48–49, 50, 52, 57
Venus, collisions **4:** 29.
See also meteoroids; meteors; micrometeorites; *and under* asteroids; iron; nickel; silicate minerals
meteoroids **4:** 55–57
asteroid origin **4:** 57
definition **4:** 11, 55
discoveries **4:** 6
Earth, collisions **4:** 10, 11
gas giant rings **5:** 7, 34, 35
Jupiter's rings **5:** 34, 35
mass **2:** 49
Mercury, bombardment **4:** 18
planet formation **4:** 9
solar system **4:** 5, 10, 40
See also meteorites; meteors; micrometeorites
meteorological satellites.
See weather satellites
meteorology **8:** 20, 24, 25, **7:** 12.
See also weather satellites

meteors **4:** 55–57
  asteroid origin **2:** 51, 52
  climate change **2:** 51, **4:** 52
  definition **4:** 11, 55
  dinosaur extinction **2:** 51, **4:** 52
  meteor craters **2:** 51. *See also*
    Meteor Crater, Arizona
  orbits **4:** 57
  "shooting stars" **4:** 11
  See also meteorites; meteoroids;
    meteor showers;
    micrometeorites
meteor showers **2:** 52, **4:** 57
Meteosat (satellite) **8:** 25
methane:
  comets **4:** 54
  gas giants **5:** 6
  Jupiter **5:** 15
  Neptune **5:** 6, 52, 53
  Pluto **4:** 44, 45, 46
  rocky planets **5:** 6
  Saturn **5:** 39
  Titan **5:** 41
  Uranus **5:** 6, 49
  See also methane-ice
methane-ice:
  comets **4:** 54
  Neptune **5:** 54
  Pluto **4:** 45
  Triton **5:** 56
Metis (Jupiter moon) **5:** 34, 35
metric (SI)/U.S. standard unit
    conversion table **all**
    volumes: 58
micrometeorites **6:** 55, **7:** 7
microwavelengths **7:** 7
microwave radiation **1:** 54, 56,
    8: 57
microwaves, energy from Sun **2:** 9
military **6:** 16, 17, 18–19, 26; **8:** 6,
    8, 28, 34
Milky Way Galaxy **1:** 4, 7, 11, 18,
    34, 37, 38, 40, 50, 51, **2:** 6–7,
    46
Mimas (Saturn moon) **5:** 36, 40, 42,
    44, 45, 46
minor planets **4:** 10, 47, 48
Mir (space station) **7:** 2, 32, 36–41,
    42, 44, 46, 53
Miranda (Uranus moon) **5:** 51
missiles. *See* ballistic missiles
M number **1:** 12, 13
molecules **1:** 14, 17, 56, **2:** 8, 21, 56,
    3: 22, 24, 44, **4:** 54, **5:** 24
Moon **2:** 50, **3:** 3, 5, 6, 8, 9, 10, 18,
    19, 24–25, 42–57, **4:** 8, 9
  age **3:** 54
  atmosphere **3:** 5, 6, 44, 45, 50,
    52, **4:** 9, **6:** 49
  axis **3:** 8, 9
  centrifugal forces **3:** 10
  density **3:** 54
  formation **2:** 54, **3:** 54, 56–57
  gravity **3:** 8, 10, 42, 44, 51, 54
  heat **3:** 44, 54, 55, 56
  inside **3:** 54–55
    asthenosphere **3:** 55
    core **3:** 54, 55
    crust **3:** 54, 55, 56
    lithosphere **3:** 55
    mantle **3:** 54, 55
    quakes **3:** 55
  landing **6:** 49–51. *See also*
    Apollo (Moon mission);
    Moon rover
  light **3:** 13, 47
  magnetism/magnetic field **3:** 55
  Mars, Moon seen from **3:** 6
  meteorite collisions **3:** 45, 52,
    48–49, 50, 57
  orbit, eccentric **3:** 8, 9, 10, 11,
    12–13, 18, 42, 54
  phases **3:** 9, 12–13
  radiation **3:** 55
  radioactive decay **3:** 44, 54
  reflect, ability to **3:** 47

Moon (*continued...*)
  size **1:** 6, **2:** 14, **3:** 19, 42
  sky, color of **3:** 44
  Sun, fragments in rock **3:** 52
  surface features **3:** 45–54
    basins **3:** 42, 46, 56
    craters **2:** 51, **3:** 42, 45, 46, 47,
      50–51, 52, 55, 56, 57, **4:** 9
    erosion **3:** 49, 50
    highlands **3:** 46, 47, 52, 54
    lava/lava flows **3:** 42, 46, 47,
      48–49, 52, 54, 55, 56
    mare (pl. maria) **3:** 42–43, 46,
      47, 52, 54, 55, **4:** 31
    mascons **3:** 54, 55
    Moon rock **3:** 52–54, 55
    mountains **3:** 50
    "soils" **3:** 44, 45, 49, 52–53
    volcanoes/volcanic activity
      3: 46, 52, 54, 55, 56
  synchronous rotation **3:** 8
  temperature **3:** 44
  tides **3:** 8–9, 10, 18
  tilt **3:** 8, 11
  See also eclipses; Ranger; *and
    under* argon; dust; glass;
    helium; hydrogen; iron;
    light; neon; potassium;
    rock; titanium; zinc
Moon rover **3:** 48–49, **6:** 51
moons (satellites):
  definition **2:** 4
  formation **2:** 54, 57, **3:** 54,
    56–57, **5:** 7, 18
  Galilean moons **5:** 8, 18, 19–34
  gas giant **2:** 50, 57, **5:** 6–7
  irregular satellites **5:** 7, 56
  Jupiter **5:** 6–7, 8, 9, 15, 16, 18–35
  Mars **4:** 42
  Neptune **5:** 6–7, 55–56
  regular satellites **5:** 7
  rocky planet **2:** 57, **4:** 8
  Saturn **5:** 6–7, 36, 40–43, 46
  shepherd satellites **5:** 41, 46, 51
  solar system **2:** 46, 47, 50
  Uranus **5:** 6–7, 48, 50–51
  See also Moon
Moulton, Forest Ray **2:** 53
Mount Everest **4:** 40, **8:** 31
mountains/mountain ranges:
  Earth **3:** 32, 33 34, 35, 36, 38, 41,
    7: 57, **8:** 30, 31, 33, 36, 38,
    42, 44, 46, 54
  Io **5:** 21
  Mercury **4:** 16, 17, 18
  Moon **3:** 50
  Venus **4:** 25, 26, 28, 29
multispectral images **8:** 33

N
NASA (National Aeronautics and
    Space Administration) **2:** 20,
    6: 17, 35, **7:** 23, 44, 46, 53, **8:** 7,
    10, 15, 20, 28, 34, 41, 44
  description **all volumes:** 2
  See also United States space
    initiatives
Navstar (satellite) **8:** 14, 15
nebula (pl. nebulae):
  cosmos **1:** 4
  formation **1:** 20
  Hubble, Edwin Powell **1:** 42
  images of **1:** 10, 11, 12, 13,
    14–15, 16, 18, 25, 26–27, 51,
    5: 4, **4:** 7, **8:** 56
  solar system origin **2:** 53, 55, 56
  See also Butterfly Nebula;
    Cat's Eye Nebula; Crab
    Nebula; Dumbbell Nebula;
    Eagle Nebula; Eskimo
    Nebula; Eta Carinae; gas
    and dust clouds; Lagoon
    Nebula; Orion Nebula;
    Stingray Nebula; *and under*
    ultraviolet radiation

neon:
  Moon **3:** 44
  solar wind **3:** 44
  See also noble gases
Neptune (planet) **2:** 46, 47, 49, 50,
    55, **4:** 5, 57, **5:** 2, 4, 6, 52–57,
    6: 55
  atmosphere **5:** 53, 54
    atmospheric pressure **5:** 54
    clouds **5:** 53, 54, 55
    storms **5:** 53, 54
    weather patterns **5:** 53, 54
    winds **5:** 53, 54
  axis **5:** 53
  centrifugal forces **5:** 53
  composition **5:** 4, 6, 55
  density **5:** 53, 55
  direction **5:** 4
  geysers **5:** 56
  gravity **5:** 5, 56
  Great Dark Spot **5:** 54
  heat **5:** 53, 54
  magnetic field **5:** 55, **6:** 55
  moons **5:** 6–7, 55–56
  orbit **2:** 47, **4:** 44, **5:** 4, 53, **6:** 56
  pressure **5:** 54
  probes. *See* Pioneer; Voyager
  radiation **5:** 53
  rings **5:** 6, 7, 55
  rotation **5:** 53
  Scooter, the **5:** 54
  seasons **5:** 53
  shape and size **5:** 4, 53
  Small Dark Spot **5:** 54
  temperature **5:** 54
  tilt **5:** 53
  See also under ammonia-ice;
    helium; hydrogen; ice,
    water; light; methane;
    methane-ice; reflect,
    ability to; rock
Nereid (Neptune moon) **5:** 55, 56
neutrinos **1:** 31, 54, **2:** 9
neutrons **1:** 30, 31, 34
neutron stars **1:** 21, 31, 33, 34, 35,
    36, **8:** 56
New General Catalogue **1:** 12, 13
New Horizons (probe) **4:** 57
new Moon **3:** 13. *See also* phases
Newton, Sir Isaac **1:** 6, **2:** 38, 53,
    4: 55, **6:** 12, 41
nickel:
  Europa **5:** 29
  meteorites **4:** 6, 57
  stars **1:** 19
Nimbus (satellite) **8:** 12–13, 20
9/11 **8:** 16, 17
nitrogen:
  auroras **2:** 45
  comets **4:** 54
  Earth **3:** 22, **5:** 41
  Mars **4:** 34
  planetary nebula **2:** 8
  Pluto **4:** 44
  spacecraft air supply **6:** 31, **7:** 34
  Sputnik sensors **6:** 23
  stars **1:** 28, 30
  Sun **2:** 17
  Titan **5:** 41, 42
  Triton **5:** 56
  Venus **4:** 23
  See also nitrogen-ice
nitrogen-ice, Triton **5:** 56
nitrogen tetroxide **6:** 11, **7:** 20
noble gases, Mars **4:** 34. *See
    also* neon
Northern Lights **3:** 21. *See
    also* auroras
nova (pl. novae) (stars) **1:** 30.
    See also supernova
nova (pl. novae) (Venus) **4:** 27
nuclear reactions, stars **1:** 23, 24,
    30, **2:** 8, 9, 10, 54. *See also*
    fusion

O
OAO (Orbiting Astronomical
    Observatory) **8:** 56
Oberon (Uranus moon) **5:** 50, 51
Oberth, Hermann **6:** 14, 16
oceans:
  Earth **2:** 10, **3:** 10, 18, 19, 27,
    28, 29, 30, 40, 41, **4:** 26, 36,
    7: 57, **8:** 20, 21, 22
  Europa **5:** 19, 29
  Ganymede **5:** 32
Oceanus Procellarum (Moon)
    3: 42–43, 46
Olympus Mons (Mars volcano)
    4: 40, 41
Oort, Jan Hendrik **4:** 55
Oort cloud **2:** 51, 52, **4:** 55
Ophelia (Uranus moon) **5:** 51
orbiter. *See* Space Shuttle
Orbiting Astronomical Observatory
    (OAO) **8:** 56
Orbiting Solar Observatory (OSO)
    8: 56
orbits:
  explained **2:** 53, 54
  first Earth orbit. *See* Sputnik
  first manned Earth orbits, *see*
    Gagarin, Yuri; Glenn, John
  geostationary **7:** 5, 25, **8:** 13
  geosynchronous **7:** 10, 12–13,
    8: 13, 14–15, 19, 23
  Kuiper belt object **2:** 52
  orbiting velocity **6:** 8, 9, 20,
    7: 10, 11, 12, 13, **8:** 13
  polar **8:** 26, 34
  quaoar **4:** 47
  satellite **1:** 9, **6:** 20, 22–24, 26,
    30, **7:** 5, 6, 12–13, **8:** 4, 6,
    10, 13, 14–15, 30, 34
  spacecraft **4:** 14, **6:** 8, 9, 33,
    34–35, 38, 41, 43, 44, 45,
    46, 47, 49, **7:** 6, 10–11, 13,
    25, 30
  See also deorbit; eccentric
    orbits; trajectory; *and
    under* asteroids; comets;
    Earth; International Space
    Station (ISS); Jupiter; Mars;
    Mercury; Moon; Neptune;
    Pluto; Saturn; stars; Sun;
    Uranus; Venus
Orientale Basin (Moon) **3:** 46
Orion Nebula **1:** 13, 17
OSO (Orbiting Solar Observatory)
    8: 56
outer planets. *See* Jupiter;
    Neptune; Pluto; Saturn;
    Uranus
oxygen:
  auroras **2:** 45
  comets **4:** 54
  Earth **3:** 5, 22, 27, 30, 39, **5:** 41
  Mars **4:** 34
  Mercury **4:** 16
  rocky planets **2:** 50, **4:** 8
  space **2:** 56
  spacecraft air supply **6:** 31, 46,
    7: 34, 41
  spacecraft fuel (liquid oxygen)
    6: 10, 11, 16, 19, 56, **7:** 14,
    15, 18, 20, 21
  stars **1:** 16, 26, 28, 29, **2:** 8
  Sun **2:** 17
ozone **2:** 41, **3:** 22, 24, **8:** 26
ozone hole **8:** 26

P
Pallas (asteroid) **4:** 10, 48, 51
Pan (Saturn moon) **5:** 40, 41, 45
Pandora (Saturn moon) **5:** 40, 45
parachutes **5:** 12, **6:** 26, 27, 33, 40,
    44, 53, **7:** 20, 28, 29
parsec, definition **1:** 11
paths. *See* orbits; trajectory
Pavonis Mons (Mars volcano) **4:** 41

payload **2**: 20, **6**: 7, 8, 9, 10, 11, 16, 18, 20, 22, **7**: 11, 15, 18, 23, 24, 25, 26. *See also* satellites; spacecraft
Payne, Cecilia **2**: 17
penumbra (eclipse) **3**: 15
penumbra (sunspot) **2**: 18, 26–27, 28
perigee **3**: 8, 14
phases:
    Earth **3**: 6
    Mercury **4**: 14
    Moon **3**: 9, 12–13
    Venus **4**: 22
Phobos (Mars moon) **4**: 42
Phoebe (Saturn Moon) **5**: 41, 45
phosphorus:
    Jupiter **5**: 15
    Saturn **5**: 40
photoevaporation **1**: 16
photons **1**: 17, 36, 46, **2**: 18, 21, 23, 38
photosphere **2**: 19, 22, 23–26, 28, 32, 33, 35, 37
photosynthesis **3**: 27
Pioneer (probe) **5**: 8, 44, **6**: 52, 54, 55, 57
Pirs (universal docking module, ISS) **7**: 44, 52, 53
planet, origin of word **1**: 9
planetary nebula **1**: 13, 21, 26–28, 29, 30–31, 33, **2**: 8, 11
planetesimals **4**: 11
planet formation:
    Earth **3**: 30, 39
    explained **2**: 49, 52–54, 56–57, **4**: 7, 8, 11, **5**: 4, 6, 34
    Jupiter **2**: 56–57, **5**: 4–5, 17, 18
    Mars **4**: 43
    other solar systems **1**: 48, 49, 57
    Saturn **5**: 17
    Uranus **2**: 54, **5**: 48, 49, 50
planets. *See* Earth; Jupiter; Mercury; Neptune; planet, origin of word; planet formation; Pluto; Saturn; Uranus; Venus
plant life **3**: 16, 27, 29, 30, **7**: 55
plasma:
    black hole **1**: 39
    comets **4**: 53
    probe **6**: 55
    Sun (solar wind) **2**: 16, 22, 26, 32, 33, 35, 38, 42, 45, 46
    See also coronal mass ejections; solar wind
plates/plate boundaries **3**: 30–37, 39, 41
Pluto **2**: 46, 47, 48, 49, 50, 51, 52, 55, **4**: 5, 7, 8, 44–47, 57, **5**: 4, 56
    atmosphere **4**: 46
    axis **4**: 45
    brightness **4**: 45
    composition **2**: 46, **4**: 44, 45
    density **4**: 45
    direction, retrograde **4**: 45
    heat **4**: 46
    moon **4**: 44, 46–47, 57
    orbit, eccentric **2**: 47, 48, 52, **4**: 7, 44, 46
    pressure **4**: 46
    rotation **4**: 45
    shape and size **4**: 5, 45
    surface features:
        basins **4**: 45
        craters **4**: 45
        polar caps **4**: 45
    synchronous rotation **4**: 46
    temperature **4**: 46
    See also under ice, water; methane; methane-ice; nitrogen; reflect, ability to; rock
polar caps:
    Ganymede **5**: 30–31
    Jupiter **5**: 16

polar caps (*continued...*)
    Mars **4**: 31, 34
    Pluto **4**: 45
    See also ice caps
pollution **7**: 57, **8**: 36, 37
Polyakov, Valery **7**: 39
Population I and II stars **1**: 19, 30
potassium:
    Mercury **4**: 16
    Moon **3**: 44
probes, space **2**: 52, **3**: 6, **6**: 4, 9, 52–57, **8**: 4. *See also* Cassini-Huygens; Galileo; Magellan; Mariner; Mars Global Surveyor; New Horizons; Pioneer; Stardust; Venera; Voyager
Progress (unmanned ferry) **7**: 32, 38, 39
projectiles. *See* rockets
Prometheus (Io volcano) **5**: 22
Prometheus (Saturn moon) **5**: 40, 45
prominences **2**: 15, 19, 33–35
propellants **6**: 7, 8, 10, 11, 12, 14, 16, 19, 20, **7**: 20, 21, 26, 33
propulsion systems **6**: 7, 9, 10, 11, 43, 55, **7**: 32. *See also* engines
Proton (rocket) **7**: 51, 52
protons **1**: 30, 34, **2**: 8, 9, 32, 33, 41, 42, 45, **3**: 19
protostars **1**: 18
Proxima Centauri (star) **1**: 11, **2**: 6, 13
pulsars **1**: 21, 33, 34, 35

Q
quantum theory **7**: 55
Quaoar (minor planet) **4**: 47
quasars **1**: 33, 35, 36, 38, **8**: 56

R
radar **7**: 26, **8**: 17, 23, 45–53
    Venus **4**: 20–21, 25, **6**: 54
    See also Shuttle Radar Topography Mission (SRTM); surveying (and mapping) Earth
radiation:
    Big Bang **1**: 54, 56
    black holes **1**: 38, 39
    comets **4**: 53
    cosmos **1**: 5
    detecting **1**: 7
    Earth **4**: 36, **8**: 26, 57
    Jupiter **5**: 15
    Mars **4**: 36
    Moon **3**: 55
    Neptune **5**: 53
    probes **6**: 55
    quasars **1**: 35
    Saturn **5**: 38
    solar (Sun) **2**: 8, 9, 10, 16–17, 22, 41, **3**: 29, **4**: 24, **5**: 6, 12, **6**: 24, **8**: 8, 26
    space **1**: 7, **2**: 8, **7**: 7
    stars **1**: 14, 20, 21, 23, 29
    universe **1**: 7, 20, 54
    Uranus **5**: 50
    Venus **4**: 25
    See also infrared; microwave radiation; synchrotron radiation; ultraviolet radiation; Van Allen belts
radiation belts. *See* Van Allen belts
radiative zone **2**: 18–19, 21, 22
radio galaxies **1**: 45
radio interference **2**: 38, 45
radioisotopes:
    power source **6**: 54, 55
    rock dating **3**: 54
radio stars **1**: 36, 45
radio telescopes **1**: 4, **2**: 8
radio waves:
    black holes **1**: 36
    Earth (ionosphere) **2**: 41, **3**: 22, **6**: 23

radio waves (*continued...*)
    Jupiter **5**: 8, 15
    pulsars **1**: 21, 34
    quasars **1**: 35
    Sun **2**: 9, 32, 46
    universe **1**: 7
    See also radar
rain (precipitation) **3**: 23, 29, **8**: 21, 22, 23, 25
Ranger (spacecraft) **6**: 53
rays, crater **3**: 46, 50, 51
reaction **2**: 38, **6**: 6, 7, 12, 41. *See also* laws of motion
red giants **1**: 21, 26, 28, 30, **2**: 10
"red planet" **4**: 6, 30
red spot (Saturn) **5**: 40
Redstone (rocket) **6**: 34, 35
reflect, ability to:
    dust and gas **8**: 54
    Earth clouds **5**: 26, 29
    Enceladus **5**: 42
    galaxies **1**: 40
    Mars **4**: 31
    Mercury **4**: 16
    Moon **3**: 47
    Neptune **5**: 53
    Pluto **4**: 45
    Triton **5**: 56
    Uranus **5**: 49
    Venus clouds **4**: 24, 25
    See also radar
relativity, theory of **1**: 46, 48, **2**: 9
remote manipulator system (RMS): International Space Station (ISS) **7**: 45, 47, 49, 52
    Space Shuttle **7**: 24, **8**: 10
remote sensing **8**: 30. *See also* surveying (and mapping) Earth
resonance **4**: 49
retroburn **6**: 45
retrograde direction:
    Pluto **4**: 45
    Triton **5**: 56
    Venus **4**: 20
retrorockets/retrofiring **6**: 31, 33, 38, 40, 43, **7**: 20, 27. *See also* retroburn
Rhea (Saturn moon) **5**: 36, 41, 45
rifts/rift valleys:
    Ariel **5**: 50
    Earth **3**: 33, **4**: 26, 41
    Mars **4**: 41
    Venus **4**: 26–27
    See also faults/fractures
rings, planet. *See under* Jupiter; Neptune; Saturn; Uranus
robotic arm. *See* remote manipulator system (RMS)
rock **2**: 56
    Callisto **5**: 30, 34
    comets **2**: 46, **4**: 54
    Earth **2**: 10, **3**: 6, 23, 28, 29, 30, 32, 34, 36, 39, 40, **4**: 41, **8**: 44, 45
    Europa **5**: 29
    Ganymede **5**: 6, 18, 30, 32
    Gaspra **4**: 10
    isotope dating **3**: 54
    Io **5**: 21, 26
    Jupiter **5**: 17
    Mars **4**: 36–37, 43
    Moon **3**: 6, 42, 44, 48–49, 52–54, 55, 56
    Neptune **5**: 6, 55
    Pluto **2**: 50, **4**: 8, 44, 45
    rocky bodies **4**: 4, 5, 6–7, 10–11, **2**: 46. *See also* asteroids; comets; interplanetary dust; meteoroids
    Saturn/Saturn's rings **5**: 7, 38, 45
    solar system **2**: 46, 56, 57
    Tethys **5**: 42
    Triton **5**: 56
    Uranus/Uranus' moons **5**: 6, 48, 49, 50, 51

rock (*continued...*)
    Venus **4**: 22, 25, 27, 29
    See also gas giant moons; lava/lava flows; rock cycle; rocky planet moons; rocky planets; sedimentary rock
rock cycle **3**: 29, 40–41
rocketry **6**: 14–21. *See also* rockets
rockets **4**: 52, **6**: 6–21, 24, 26, 27, 31, 34, 35, 40, 41, 42–43, 44, 45, 46, 49, 56, **7**: 14, 17, 22, **8**: 6–7, 10, 13, 14, 29–30
    aerodynamic design **6**: 7, 16, 22, **7**: 17
    lift/lifting force **6**: 9, 24, 46, **7**: 9, 14, 17, **8**: 10
    See also Agena (rocket); booster pods; engines; launchers/launch vehicles; propellants; propulsion systems; Proton (rocket); Redstone (rocket); retrorockets; rocketry; takeoffs; thrusters; Viking program (rockets)
rocky planet moons **2**: 57. *See also* Moon; *and under* Earth; Mars; Mercury; Pluto
rocky planets **2**: 50, **4**: 4 *and throughout*, **5**: 6
    formation **2**: 56–57, **4**: 7, 8
    See also Earth; Mars; Mercury; Pluto; Venus
Russell, Henry Norris **2**: 10
Russia **6**: 14, 18, **7**: 4, 30, 44, 45, 52, **8**: 25, 37, 38
Russian Space Agency **7**: 52
Russian space initiatives **3**: 54, **6**: 18, 30, **7**: 4, 30, 44, 46, **8**: 9. *See also* International Space Station (ISS); Mir; Salyut; Soyuz; Sputnik; Venera; Vostok

S
Salyut (space station) **7**: 30–32, 33, 36, 38, 42
sand dunes:
    Earth **8**: 36
    Mars **4**: 36
    Venus **4**: 24
Saros cycle **3**: 14
satellites (man-made) **1**: 9, **2**: 20–21, 42, **6**: 8, 9, 17, 20, 22–29, 30, **7**: 4, 5, 6–7, 16, 17, 25, **8**: 4 *and throughout*
    astronomical **8**: 54–57
    communications **6**: 28–29, **7**: 5, 6–7, 12, 13, **8**: 4, 7, 8, 13, 14–15, 17
    cost **8**: 6–7, 10, 15
    design **6**: 23, 28, **7**: 6–7, 9
    formation **8**: 14–15
    geostationary **6**: 28, **8**: 7, 14, 23, 26
    geosynchronous **7**: 12, 13
    global positioning system (GPS) **6**: 23, **7**: 5, **8**: 4, 7, 13, 14
    inertial upper stage (Space Shuttle) **7**: 25
    military **8**: 6, 8, 34
    polar-orbiting **7**: 13, **8**: 13, 26, 34
    reflecting **8**: 8, 9
    telephone **8**: 4, 7, 8
    television **8**: 4, 7
    weather **6**: 27–28, **7**: 12, **8**: 4, 14, 17, 20–27
    See also Aqua; COBE; Discoverer; Echo; ERTS-1; Explorer; GOES; Grace; Hubble Space Telescope; INTELSAT VI; Landsat; Meteosat; Navstar; Nimbus; SOHO; Sputnik; Syncom;

satellites (man-made) (continued...)
Terra; Telstar; Tiros;
and under centrifugal
forces; infrared
satellites (natural). *See* moons
(satellites)
Saturn (launcher) 6: 4–5, 11, 17, 20,
43, 7: 33, 34
Saturn (planet) 1: 9, 2: 46, 47, 49,
50, 55, 3: 19, 4: 4, 5: 2, 4, 5,
6–7, 17, 36–47, 6: 52, 54, 55,
56, 57
atmosphere 5: 37, 38, 39–40
clouds 5: 38, 39, 40
weather patterns 5: 38
winds 5: 38, 39
axis 5: 37
centrifugal forces 5: 39
composition 5: 4, 6, 37–39
density 2: 50, 5: 37
direction 5: 4
formation 5: 17
gravity/gravitational field 5: 6,
39, 45, 46
heat 5: 38
magnetic field 5: 37, 38, 6: 55
mass 5: 37
moons 5: 6–7, 36, 40–43, 46
orbit 2: 47; 5: 4, 36, 6: 56
pressure 5: 38, 39
probes. *See* Cassini-Huygens;
Pioneer; Voyager
radiation 5: 38
radius/radii (Rs) 5: 45
red spot 5: 40
rings 5: 6, 7, 36–37, 40, 44–47
rotation 5: 37
shape and size 3: 19, 5: 5, 36, 37,
38, 39
star, potential to be 5: 37
temperature 5: 39
tilt 5: 37
See also under ammonia;
ammonia-ice; helium;
hydrogen; ice; water;
metallic hydrogen;
methane; phosphorus; rock
Saturn radii (Rs) 5: 45
Schirra, Jr., Walter M. 6: 35
Scooter, the (Neptune) 5: 54
seasons:
Earth 3: 10–11, 8: 19
Mars 4: 32
Neptune 5: 53
sediment 3: 34, 41, 8: 41
sedimentary rock 3: 29, 41
seismic waves:
earthquake 3: 38
"moon" quakes 3: 55
sensors 1: 7, 6: 23, 8: 8, 15, 16–19,
20, 24, 25, 26, 33, 34, 37, 54, 56
Shepard, Alan B. 6: 34–35
shepherd satellites 5: 41, 46, 51
shock waves:
Big Bang 1: 56
bow 2: 40, 41, 42
solar 2: 32, 33, 41
Shoemaker-Levy 9 (comet) 4: 53
shooting stars. *See* meteoroids;
meteors
Shuttle. *See* Space Shuttle
Shuttle Radar Topography Mission
(SRTM) 8: 46–53
sidereal month 3: 8–9
Sif Mons (Venus) 4: 28, 29
silicate minerals:
Earth 3: 39
meteorites 4: 57
"stardust" 4: 10
silica tiles (ISS) 7: 28
silicon:
Earth 3: 39
rocky planets 4: 8
space 2: 56
stars 1: 14, 30
Sun 2: 17

sky, picture of entire 1: 4–5
Skylab (space station) 2: 31,
7: 30-31, 33–35, 36, 42, 44
slingshot/slingshot trajectory 4: 14,
54, 6: 52, 55, 56, 57
Small Dark Spot (Neptune) 5: 54
snow:
Earth 3: 6, 23, 28, 29, 8: 25,
30, 38
Mars 4: 34
sodium:
Mercury 4: 16
Sun 2: 16
universe 1: 14
SOHO (Solar and Heliospheric
Observatory) satellite 2: 20–21
"soils":
Earth 3: 39, 40
Gaspra (asteroid) 4: 10
Mars 4: 34, 43
Mercury 4: 17
Moon 3: 44, 45, 49, 52–53
Venus 4: 25
solar arrays. *See* solar panels
solar cells 6: 25, 26, 28, 29, 7: 50,
8: 19. *See also* solar panels
solar eclipses 3: 14, 15
solar flares 2: 19, 24, 32–33, 35, 45
solar nebula 2: 54
solar panels (arrays) 2: 20, 6: 52,
7: 6, 7, 32, 33, 34, 35, 36, 38,
42, 52, 8: 14, 20, 57. *See also*
solar cells
solar prominences 2: 15, 19, 33–35
solar quake 2: 32
solar radiation. *See under* radiation
solar sail 2: 38–39
solar system 2: 2, 46–57, 4: 4, 5, 5: 4
age 3: 54, 4: 11, 5: 4
composition 2: 4, 46, 49–52,
3: 44, 4: 54
diagram 2: 48–49, 4: 4–5
formation 2: 10, 52–57, 4: 10, 11
mass 2: 4, 14, 49
organization 2: 48, 49
solar wind 2: 4, 9, 11, 20, 33, 37,
38–45, 46, 3: 20, 21, 24, 44, 52,
6: 54, 7: 7, 56, 8: 56
comets 4: 54
discovery 4: 54
heliosphere 2: 40, 41
Mercury 4: 16
Moon 3: 44, 52
Uranus 5: 50
Venus 4: 22
See also auroras;
magnetospheres; stellar
wind; *and under* neon
sonic boom 4: 57, 7: 29
Southern Cross (Crux) 1: 8
Southern Lights 3: 21. *See also*
auroras
South Pole-Aitken Basin (Moon)
3: 46
Soviet space initiatives. *See* Russian
space initiatives
Soviet Union, former 6: 14, 18, 19,
22, 24, 26, 30, 33, 38, 7: 4, 30,
32, 44, 8: 8
Soyuz (ferry) 6: 18, 33, 7: 32–33, 38,
39, 44, 45
space, Sun's corona 2: 35
spacecraft 2: 20, 38, 6: 4 *and
throughout*, 7: 4 *and
throughout*
capsules 6: 26, 27, 30, 33, 34, 35,
37, 38, 41, 44, 51, 7: 32, 35
design 7: 6–7, 9, 17
ejection seats 6: 31, 33, 40
future development 7: 56
gimbals 6: 12, 13, 16, 7: 20, 25
hatches, entry and exit 6: 40, 41,
7: 56–57
heat shields 5: 12, 6: 26, 33, 40,
44, 46, 51, 7: 27, 8: 57
nose cones 6: 7, 10, 22

spacecraft (continued...)
recovering 6: 26, 30, 35, 41, 51;
7: 20, 23, 8: 15
trusses 6: 52, 7: 45, 52, 53
See also Apollo (Moon
mission); docking,
spacecraft; engines; fuel,
spacecraft; Gemini; lunar
module; Mercury; probes,
space; Progess; Ranger;
retrorockets; rockets;
Space Shuttle; Viking
mission (Mars); Vostok;
and under centrifugal
forces; hydrogen; nitrogen;
oxygen
spaceflight, manned. *See* manned
spaceflight
Spacehab 7: 24
Spacelab 7: 24
space probes. *See* probes, space
space race 6: 19, 22–29, 7: 4
Space Shuttle (Space
Transportation System (STS))
6: 11, 13, 7: 4, 8, 9, 13, 14–29,
36–37, 38, 40–41, 44, 46, 8: 4,
10, 45, 48–49, 50
boosters 6: 11, 7: 8–9, 14, 15, 17,
18–20, 21
external tank 6: 11, 7: 8–9, 14,
15, 17, 18, 19, 20, 21
orbiter 6: 11, 7: 14, 15, 17, 18,
19, 20–23, 24, 25, 26, 27–29
See also Atlantis; Challenger;
Columbia; Discovery;
Endeavour; Enterprise;
inertial upper stage;
Shuttle Radar Topography
Mission (SRTM)
space stations 7: 4, 6, 13, 17,
30, 32, 36, 42. *See also*
International Space Station
(ISS); Mir; Salyut; Skylab
Space Transportation System (STS).
See Space Shuttle
spacewalking. *See* extravehicular
activity
spicules 2: 33, 35
Sputnik (satellite) 6: 18, 22–24, 26,
8: 8, 9, 30
SRTM (Shuttle Radar Topography
Mission) 8: 46–47, 48, 50,
52–53
Stardust (probe) 4: 54
"stardust." *See* interplanetary dust
stars 1: 7, 8–9, 14–39
atmosphere 1: 26, 2: 53
brightness 1: 18, 21, 24, 30, 33.
See also magnitude
cataloguing 1: 12
classification 1: 19
clusters (open and globular)
1: 12, 19–20, 8: 57
elements. *See under* calcium;
carbon; helium; hydrogen;
iron; nickel; nitrogen;
oxygen; silicon; sulfur
energy 1: 21, 23, 26, 30, 31,
35, 45
formation 1: 14–18, 38
fuel 1: 21, 23, 24, 26, 29, 2: 8–9
gravity/gravitational field 1: 18,
19, 20, 23, 24, 26, 29, 30,
31, 42, 56, 2: 8, 9
heat 1: 18, 20, 21, 23, 26, 29
life cycle 1: 14–15, 19, 20–33,
2: 10–11, 8: 57
light 1: 16, 18, 24, 29, 30, 33,
39, 42, 45
magnetic field 1: 34
magnitude 2: 13, 8: 56
near-star event 2: 53
nuclear reactions 1: 23, 24, 30,
2: 8, 9, 10, 54
orbit 1: 42
pressure 1: 18

stars (continued...)
radiation 1: 14, 20, 21, 23, 29
rotation in galaxy 1: 42
temperature 1: 21
twinkling effect 8: 54
See also Betelgeuse (star); binary
stars; black dwarf stars;
blue giants; DG Tau (star);
dwarf stars; main-sequence
stars; neutron stars; nova;
Population I and II stars;
protostars; Proxima Centauri
(star); pulsars; radio stars;
Sun; supernova; T-Tauri
stars; white dwarf stars; *and
under* infrared; ultraviolet
light
stellar winds 1: 14, 18, 25, 26, 28,
51, 2: 40. *See also* solar wind
Stingray Nebula 2: 8
stratosphere 3: 22, 24
STS. *See* Space Shuttle
subduction zones 3: 32, 33, 34,
36–37
sulfur:
comets 4: 54
Earth 3: 39
Io 5: 21, 23, 24
Jupiter 5: 14, 15
stars 1: 16, 30
sulfur dioxide, Io 5: 22, 26
sulfuric acid clouds, Venus 4: 20,
23, 24
Sun 1: 5, 6, 7, 11, 19, 24, 42, 2: 2, 4,
6, 7, 8–9, 10–11, 12–45, 46, 48,
53, 54, 4: 57, 6: 54
age 2: 10
atmosphere 2: 12, 18, 20, 22–37
chromosphere 2: 18, 22, 32,
33, 35
corona 2: 19, 22, 35–37, 38,
41, 53, 3: 15
coronal loops 2: 35, 36–37
coronal mass ejections 2: 4–5,
22–23, 35, 44
flares 2: 19, 24, 32–33, 35, 45
photosphere 2: 19, 22, 23–26,
28, 32, 33, 35, 37
prominences 2: 15, 19, 33–35
spicules 2: 33, 35
storms 2: 33, 42–43, 44–45
axis 2: 13, 24, 47
birth 2: 8, 10
brightness 1: 24, 2: 9, 10, 11,
12–13, 16
death 2: 10–11
density 2: 11, 16, 22, 23
"diamond ring" 3: 14–15
Earth, distance from 2: 12
elements 2: 16–17. *See also
under* calcium; carbon;
helium; hydrogen; iron;
magnesium; nitrogen;
oxygen; silicon; sodium
energy 2: 8–9, 16, 21, 22, 28, 31,
32, 33, 38, 46, 3: 22, 28, 8: 26
fuel 2: 8–9
gravity 2: 8, 9, 14, 16, 46, 3: 10,
8: 56
heat 2: 21, 22, 32, 41, 46, 54
heliopause 2: 40, 41
helioseismology 2: 16, 32
heliosphere 2: 40–41, 44, 45
heliotail 2: 40
inside:
convective zone 2: 18–19,
22, 23
core 2: 8, 16, 18–19, 21
radiative zone 2: 18–19, 21, 22
light 2: 6, 9, 11, 16–17, 21, 23,
24, 32, 41, 46, 3: 11, 13,
14–15, 22
magnetism/magnetic field 2: 16,
28, 32, 33, 35, 37, 41, 42–45,
46
mass 2: 4, 9, 14, 22

Sun (continued...)
  modeling to test theories 2: 16
  orbit 1: 37, 8: 26
  pressure 6: 8, 16
  probes 6: 54. See also Orbiting
    Solar Observatory; SOHO
    satellite
  quakes and vibrations 2: 16, 32
  radiation, solar 2: 8, 9, 10,
    16–17, 22, 41, 3: 29, 4: 24,
    5: 6, 12, 6: 24, 8: 8, 26
  radio waves 2: 9, 32, 46
  radius 2: 16, 21
  rotation 2: 12–13, 24, 26
  size 1: 6, 2: 14, 15, 36–37
  star type 1: 19, 2: 12
  surface features:
    granulation 2: 24, 26–27, 28
    sunspots 2: 12–13, 26–32, 35
  temperature 2: 10, 12, 22, 23,
    26, 28, 32, 35, 40
  tilt 2: 13
  See also auroras; eclipses; solar
    sail; solar wind; tides; and
    under convection currents;
    infrared; plasma; ultraviolet
    light; ultraviolet radiation
sunspots 2: 12–13, 26–32, 35
supernova (pl. supernovae)
  1: 13, 21, 30, 31–33, 34, 51,
  8: 54–55, 56
solar system origin 2: 54
surveying (and mapping) Earth
  6: 23, 7: 4, 13, 26, 8: 13, 14.
  See also global positioning
  system; Landsat; radar;
  remote sensing; Shuttle Radar
  Topography Mission (SRTM);
  triangulation
synchronous orbit, Charon 4: 46
synchronous rotation:
  Charon 4: 46
  Io 5: 26
  Moon 3: 8
  Venus 4: 22
synchrotron radiation 1: 39
Syncom (satellite) 8: 14
synodic month 3: 9
synodic period 4: 15

T
takeoffs 6: 4, 11, 24, 7: 9, 10–11, 13
  Apollo 6: 10, 42–43, 44, 45, 47
  Cassini/Titan 6: 21
  Friendship 7 (Mercury) 6: 36
  Gemini 6: 38
  Proton (International Space
    Station) 7: 51
  Space Shuttle 7: 14, 17, 18–19,
    20, 21, 22, 23, 26–27, 29,
    8: 9
  See also rockets
tectonic plates. See plates
telecommunications 7: 56. See also
  telephone
telephone 8: 4, 7, 8. See also
  telecommunications
telescopes 1: 6, 7, 12, 4: 49, 5: 18,
  7: 34, 8: 15, 54–57. See also
  Hubble Space Telescope; radio
  telescopes
Telesto (Saturn moon) 5: 40, 41
television (satellite) 6: 25, 27, 28,
  29, 8: 4, 7, 13, 14. See also
  Telstar; Tiros
Telstar (satellite) 6: 28–29, 8: 8
Tereshkova, Valentina 6: 35
Terra (satellite) 8: 14–15, 27, 41, 44
Tethys (Saturn moon) 5: 36, 40, 42,
  43, 45
Tharsis (Mars) 4: 41
Thebe (Jupiter moon) 5: 34, 35
theory of relativity 1: 46, 48, 2: 9
thermal imaging 8: 40–44
thermosphere 3: 22, 24
Thor (launcher) 6: 19

thrusters (orientation rockets)
  6: 40, 7: 38, 39
tidal effect 5: 22
tides:
  Earth 3: 8–9, 10, 18
  Moon 3: 18
time machine, light as 1: 50, 53
Tiros (satellite) 6: 27–28, 8: 17,
  20, 26
Titan (launcher) 6: 19, 21, 38, 56
Titan (Saturn moon) 2: 50, 5: 36,
  41–42, 45, 6: 57
Titania (Uranus moon) 5: 50, 51
titanium:
  Mercury 4: 18
  Moon 3: 52
Titov, German 6: 33
topography 5: 41, 8: 43–50. See
  also Shuttle Radar Topography
  Mission (SRTM)
total eclipse 2: 33, 3: 14
trajectory 6: 9, 34, 43, 44, 47, 52,
  56, 7: 10–11, 20. See also
  slingshot trajectory
transponders 8: 14, 17, 19
triangulation 8: 48–49, 51
Triton (Neptune moon) 4: 47, 5: 55,
  56, 57
tropical cyclones 8: 22. See also
  hurricanes
troposphere 3: 22, 24, 28
trusses 6: 52, 7: 45, 52, 53
Tsiolkovsky, Konstantin
  Eduardovich 6: 14, 16
T-Tauri stars 1: 18, 48
Tycho Brahe 1: 6
Tycho impact basin 3: 42–43
typhoons. See hurricanes

U
ultraviolet light:
  satellite sensors 8: 26, 56
  stars 1: 16, 17, 22–23
  Sun 2: 9, 16–17, 32, 37, 41
  See also photons
ultraviolet radiation:
  Earth 3: 22, 24
  nebula 1: 51
  Sun 2: 33, 41
umbra (eclipse) 3: 15
umbra (sunspot) 2: 18, 26–27, 28
Umbriel (Uranus moon) 5: 50, 51
United States, first photo map
  8: 28–29
United States space initiatives
  6: 24–26, 30, 7: 4, 44, 45, 46.
  See also Apollo; Gemini; GOES;
  International Space Station;
  Mercury; NASA; probes, space;
  Skylab
Unity (ISS) 7: 42–43, 45, 50, 51, 52
universe 1: 4, 6, 40, 46–57, 2: 6
  age 1: 20, 42, 54
  composition 1: 14, 17, 19, 2: 6,
    17, 56, 4: 54. See also under
    calcium; helium; hydrogen;
    sodium; water
  continuation 1: 57
  expanding 1: 42, 53–57
  "observable" 1: 53
  origin 1: 6, 42, 54, 55, 56, 8: 57
  structure 1: 49–50
  See also Cosmological Principle;
    and under energy; light;
    radiation; radio waves;
    X-rays
Uranus (planet) 2: 46, 47, 48, 49, 50,
  55, 4: 5, 5: 2, 4, 6, 48–51, 6: 55
  atmosphere 5: 49
    auroras 5: 50
    clouds 5: 48
    winds 5: 49
  axis 5: 48, 49
  centrifugal forces 5: 49
  color 5: 49
  density 5: 48

Uranus (continued...)
  direction 5: 4, 48
  formation 5: 48, 49, 50, 2: 54
  gravitational field 5: 49, 50
  heat 5: 50
  inside 5: 4, 6, 49, 50
  magnetic field 5: 49, 50, 6: 55
  mass 5: 50
  moons 5: 6–7, 48, 50–51
  orbit 2: 47, 4: 44, 5: 4, 48, 6: 56
  pressure 5: 50
  probes. See Pioneer, Voyager
  radiation 5: 50
  rings 5: 6, 7, 48, 50, 51
  rotation 5: 48, 49
  shape and size 5: 4, 48, 49
  tilt, extreme 2: 48, 54
  See also under ammonia;
    ammonia-ice; energy;
    helium; hydrogen; ice;
    water; methane; reflect,
    ability to; rock; water
Ursa Major (Great Bear) 1: 8
U.S. standard unit/metric
  (SI) conversion table all
  volumes: 58

V
V1/V2 (Vengeance weapons) 6: 16,
  8: 29
vacuum 2: 23, 7: 7, 17, 56
Valles Marineris (Mars) 4: 39, 41
Van Allen, Dr. James 6: 24
Van Allen belts 3: 19, 24, 6: 24
Vanguard (launcher) 6: 19, 24
Vanguard (satellite) 6: 24, 26
Venera (probe) 6: 53
Venus (planet) 2: 10, 42, 46, 47,
  48, 50, 55, 4: 2, 4, 5, 6, 20–29,
  6: 52, 53, 54, 56
  atmosphere 3: 27, 4: 20, 23–25,
    29
    atmospheric pressure 4: 23
    clouds, sulfuric acid 4: 20, 22,
      23, 24, 25
    "greenhouse" effect 4: 24–25
    winds 4: 24
  axis 4: 20
  brightness 4: 20, 24
  centrifugal forces 4: 22
  death 2: 10
  density 4: 22
  direction, retrograde 4: 20
  heat 4: 25, 6: 53
  inside:
    convection currents 4: 29
    core 4: 29
    crust 4: 26, 27, 28, 29
    mantle 4: 29
    plates 4: 26, 29
  mass 4: 22
  orbit 2: 47, 4: 7, 20, 22, 6: 57
  probes. See Magellan; Mariner;
    Pioneer; Venera
  radiation 4: 25
  radioactive decay 4: 29
  rotation 4: 20, 22
  shape and size 4: 5, 22
  surface features 4: 20–21, 25–29
    basins 4: 26
    calderas 4: 29
    chasm 4: 26
    corona 4: 27
    craters 4: 25, 28, 29
    depressions 4: 29
    faults/fractures 4: 26–27, 28
    highlands 4: 27
    lava/lava flows 4: 25, 26, 27,
      28, 29
    mountains 4: 25, 26, 28, 29
    nova 4: 27
    plains 4: 25, 26, 27
    plateaus 4: 26
    ridges 4: 25, 26
    rifts/rift valleys 4: 26–27
    sand dunes 4: 24

Venus (continued...)
  scarp 4: 26–27
  "soils" 4: 25
  volcanoes/volcanic activity
    4: 25, 27, 28–29
  synchronous rotation 4: 22
  temperature 4: 25
  See also under carbon dioxide;
    magma; nitrogen; phases;
    radar; rock
Vesta (asteroid) 4: 10, 48, 51
Viking mission (Mars) 4: 36–37,
  38–39
Viking program (rockets) 8: 29
volcanoes/volcanic activity:
  Earth 3: 27, 30, 32, 33, 38, 39,
    40, 41, 7: 57, 8: 38–39,
    46–47
  Enceladus 5: 6–7, 42
  Io 2: 50, 5: 15, 19, 20–24, 26, 35.
    See also Prometheus
  Mars 4: 38, 40, 41, 43. See also
    Albor Tholus; Ascraeus
    Mons; Ascraeus Mons;
    Elysium Mons; Hecates
    Tholus; Olympus Mons;
    Pavonis Mons
  Moon 3: 46, 52, 54, 55, 56
  Venus 4: 25, 27, 28–29
von Braun, Wernher 6: 16–17, 7: 42
Vostok 6: 18, 30, 31, 33, 34, 35
Voyager (space probe) 2: 6, 5: 8,
  18, 19, 21, 26–27, 36, 44, 45,
  46, 49, 50, 55, 6: 52, 54–56

W
water:
  Callisto 5: 18, 19
  Earth 3: 16, 22, 23, 27, 28, 29
  Europa 5: 29
  Ganymede 5: 18, 19, 30, 32
  Jupiter 5: 15
  Mars 4: 31, 33, 34, 40, 41
  Miranda 5: 51
  solar system origin 2: 56–57
  universe, most common
    molecule in 2: 56
  Uranus 5: 48, 49
  See also ice, water; water cycle;
    water vapor
water cycle 3: 24, 28, 29, 32, 36, 40
water-ice. See ice, water
water vapor:
  comets 4: 53
  Earth 3: 22, 23, 28, 29, 39, 8: 2,
    22, 24, 25
  Mars 4: 32, 34, 36, 40
weapons, atomic 6: 18. See also
  ballistic missiles
weather satellites 6: 27–28, 7: 12,
  8: 4, 14, 17, 20–27
weathering 3: 46, 50, 4: 25.
  See also erosion
weightlessness 6: 16, 7: 42, 57
Whirlpool Galaxy 1: 44–45
white dwarf stars 1: 21, 29, 32,
  2: 11, 3: 33
woman, first in space 6: 35

X
X-rays:
  black holes 1: 35, 36, 8: 56
  cosmos 1: 5, 7
  galaxies 1: 45
  neutron stars 8: 56
  pulsars 1: 34
  quasars 1: 35
  space, first detection in 8: 56
  Sun 2: 9, 32, 33, 41
  supernova 8: 56
  universe 1: 5, 7

Z
Zarya (ISS) 7: 42–43, 45, 50, 51, 52
zinc, Moon 3: 52
Zvezda service module (ISS)
  7: 44, 52